Winning Through

A Loss

A BOOK OF HOPE

Jason Faulstich

Contents

ACKNOWLEDGEMENTS

God, You placed it upon my heart to write this book and I owe You so much for all that You have done for me. Without You I am a bumbling fool. With You, anything is possible. Thank You for sticking by my side even when I think I can do it on my own and for loving me enough to die for me.

I also owe a huge thanks to my amazing wife Fawn for not only helping with the book but for making my life far more beautiful and fun. Without you, this book would not have happened. You encouraged and supported me during the entire writing process and gave me countless ideas on how to improve the book. Thank you for saying yes.

I would also like to thank all of my readers that gave me feedback before it was a finished project. Christina Forsyth, Bobbie Lancaster, and Becky Shelly McFadden, your help and contributions to the book are immeasurable and I appreciate the time you took from your busy schedules to read it and provide feedback.

PREFACE

On June 27, 2006 my wife Kari died unexpectedly and my life was turned upside down. It wasn't long after she died, that God placed it upon my heart to write this book. I had always wanted to write a book but I can tell you for sure, I never expected it to be about my life. But really, this story isn't about my life. It is about the power of God.

During the writing process, I was constantly reminded of the pain from my past. To be truthful, I had buried a lot of it away like trash in a landfill, to be forgotten forever. This book forced me to relive many painful memories and has no doubt caused a few tear drops to fall. These tear drops however, are not tear drops of a broken heart or tear drops of unsettled grief. My tears fell out of my love for God and all that He did for me during my grief. As I relived my past, I was reminded of Gods' love and God's strength. I was overcome with emotion when I recalled what He did in my life when I needed him so desperately. How quickly we can forget the details from our past, when we are struggling to keep up with the present, and at the same time, always looking ahead to the future. It's easy to lose track of where we have been.

This book is not intended to be a grief book. This is a book of hope and a book of victory. This is a story about life. It is about the rollercoaster that we ride every day. Some days are filled with joy and laughter. Other days are filled with pain and tears. Unfortunately, there is nothing we can do to make life be filled with rainbows and unicorns. We live in a sinful world and that makes life downright hard.

Life can be described as a race. There is a beginning, an end, and lots of busyness, pain, and excitement in between. Like a race, life is over not long after you start it. Some don't even make it to their first pit stop before they succumb. We run here and there and get so busy, we forget about what's important. At times, we forget why we are even running. In Corinthians 9: 24-27, Paul also compares life to a race. *24 "Do you not know that in a race all the runners run, but only one gets the prize? Run in such a way as to get the prize. 25 Everyone who competes in the games goes into strict training. They do it to get a crown that will not last, but we do it to get a crown that will last forever. 26 Therefore I do not run like someone running aimlessly; I do not fight like a boxer beating the air. 27 No, I strike a blow to my body and make it my slave so that after I have preached to others, I myself will not be disqualified for the prize."* It's important to not just run the race, but run the race with purpose.

When I was deep in my grief, God taught me many things. For the first time in my life, at least since I was a child, I had no place to be and nothing to do. It was during this down time, that I heard him speaking to me because I had time to listen. It was probably the same things he had been trying to teach me all along but because of the race I was running, I didn't hear him. I bought into the 'American dream' lie that acquiring stuff, makes you happy. I wanted the big house, the green grass, and the nice things. I was running the race as fast as I could but I was not winning. I quickly learned after my wife died that stuff did not matter. In an instant, I had a paradigm shift that has forever changed me. I realized that no amount of things could bring me joy. It was the little things in life that mattered; Things that money can't buy like faith, hope, purpose, and love.

While walking through the valley of grief was so very difficult to go through, I am thankful for my experiences of my past for I am not sure I would have ever been awoken from the deep slumber I was in, had it not happened. I will forever have scars from what I experienced but I would not be who I am today, had it not been for what I went through.

The scars that I carry around, serve as my reminder of the pain that I endured and the grace that God gives me. They remind me to stay focused on what truly matter in this life, a life that is sometimes far too short. It is my hope that this book, not only can give comfort to some that may be dealing with difficult times in their lives, but it would also awaken others that are living the life that I once did.

Psalm 128:2
You will eat the fruit of your labor; blessings
and prosperity will be yours. (NIV)

CHAPTER 1

THE DREAM

I have had the dream for as long as I can remember. My dream was not just to own any piece of land. I wanted a large wooded property. I envisioned it to be a place to hunt, a place to hike, a place to escape life's stress and pressure. I began working toward that dream shortly after my wife Kari and I got married.

Ever since I was a child, having my own land was all I thought about. I dreamed about it. I daydreamed about it. It consumed me. I grew up in a town where there were no woods. Only corn fields for as far as you could see. My parents often took us kids camping and hiking and I would come alive whenever I stepped foot into the woods. It was a magical place with endless possibilities. It is where I felt at home.

Kari and I got married on May 3, 1997 in the small church in Elwood Indiana, that Kari grew up in. At that time I was making seven dollars an hour and she was making a whole five dollars. We pinched every penny we had, yet we still managed to just get by. Our passion and our drive had us wanting more. I had always been pretty good with my hands and I enjoyed building things. Our plan was to buy a house, fix it up, sell it, and then reinvest into a better one.

Our first house cost a mere 35,500 dollars, was a dreadful puke green color, and the back half of the house had no foundation. With the help of Kari's father and grandfather, we replaced the back section of the house. The framing of the new addition took one week but it took several more weeks of long, tiresome days, to finish the project. The new addition had a laundry room, a master bedroom, and master bath. After the room addition was complete, much more work had to be done on the rest of the house. New roofing, siding, trim, doors, carpeting, and painting. In the midst of all the work, our first child, Lauren was born.

The work was constant for two years before our first house was finished. I grew tired during the renovation process but I always kept the dream alive in my mind. It drove me to keep going. What does any rational person do after fixing up a house and getting it just the way they want it? We placed it for sale. Within one month of being on the market, it sold. On to the next one we went.

The second house was a much larger project. The two story, 100 year old house had been turned into two apartments. There was one apartment downstairs and one apartment upstairs with an outside staircase. I dedicated the next year to completely renovating the home. It financially stretched us a bit, but we rented a house in town while demolition took place.   As soon as the house was gutted, I lost my job. With two housing payments and no job, our backs were against the wall. The mountain of debt began piling up. Things we had taken for granted like having food in the kitchen cabinets, was a thing of the past. We started selling things. We just tried to survive.

All the while, I had an incredibly large task ahead of me. I had to tear out walls, build new walls, drywall, add all new subflooring, put on a new roof, add siding, rewire the entire house, add all new windows, rebuild the porch floor, and build an open staircase to the second level. I became worn out and exhausted working 12 hour days, seven days a week, at the house. When the house was nearly completed, I landed a job in town. It wasn't a good job but it allowed us to pay some bills.

After one full year of devoting every ounce of sweat I had, the house was complete. It had been transformed from what once was a dilapidated house that looked inches from finding its eternal resting place, to a beautiful new home that one realtor even called, "One of the nicest homes in town." Kari and I were so very proud of that house and how we had changed it so much, but we wouldn't rest long. It wasn't a year later and another job change had us moving again.

With my new job now 90 minutes away in Lafayette, we relocated to a town South West of Lafayette called Williamsport. We settled there after looking for a reasonably priced place to live within easy driving distance to work. Williamsport was the county seat but it was a very small town of 1800 people, and there weren't any towns nearby. The entire county had only one stoplight and it served no purpose but to use electricity as it just flashed yellow. Williamsport was the kind of place you were expecting to see tumble weeds blowing through at any time and a few times I think I did. After being extremely worn out from all that we done thus far, we opted to have a house built for us. We decided to rent a small duplex just down the road as construction took place.

The construction of the new house took what seemed like forever as for once, we sat by idle. Finally, after six long months, the wait was over. We were both thrilled and ecstatic that move in day had arrived. The house was a three bedroom, 1500 square foot, brick, ranch style with an open concept and vaulted ceilings. The kitchen and living room were separated by a small wall with a wood burning fireplace. I put my touch on things by building a fireplace mantel and surround shortly after moving in. Kari liked our new house, but she did not like the rural location. This move took us both away from our home town for the first time in our lives. She felt extremely isolated and never felt at home there. I loved it there with all that it had to offer for an outdoorsman. I had always been passionate about deer hunting and the place was filled with them. I had just recently shot the biggest deer of my life, a deer that got my name in the Pope and Young Club Record Book. I knew the chances of shooting another big one there were pretty good.

Although Kari never felt at home in Williamsport, she did find a new passion and hobby while there........ginseng hunting. Her new friend in town turned her onto it and she quickly fell in love. She loved the mystery of at first, having to find a plant, and then having to dig the root up, never knowing how big it was going to be. We sold the roots that we gathered up the road to a local buyer. We didn't make a lot of money but it was never about the money. She just loved the adventure.

With Kari's unhappiness in Williamsport, I had been contemplating moving for a while. It was an extremely hard choice, but my love for my wife and my passion for my dream, had us moving again. Kari had recently found out she was pregnant with our second child so now seemed like the perfect time to uproot and find our home. We placed our home on the market and one month later, it sold.

We looked around and decided to move to Lafayette. We looked at houses for a while but just didn't find anything that we liked for the money. We decided we would be better off building our own house again, only this time, we would do the work. We found a small property seven miles out of town. It was a 3 ½ acre soybean field. Even though the property didn't have a single tree on it, there was quite a bit of woods around in every direction. It was more land than I had ever owned, and Kari would be closer to shopping and she would have more opportunities to be social. Building there just made sense.

Kari gave me her wish list for her new house, we bought a computer program, and I drew up the floor plan and exterior design. Just a few short months later, we broke ground. We lived at Kari's parents in Elwood for six weeks and commuted back and forth during early construction. It was about an 80 minute trip each way and the days were long. Framing was complete in two weeks with the help of a friend, Kari's uncle, and Kari's father. I had a coworker volunteer to do the heating and cooling if I bought the materials so I accepted his help without hesitation. I hired out the drywall, plumbing, and some brickwork but I did all the rest. The next five months were spent wiring, insulating, painting, hanging cabinets, handing doors, putting up trim, and tiling floors. During this time we also moved from Kari's parents' house to a rental house in Lafayette. We stayed in the two bedroom rental house for four months as construction was completed.

The building process was exhausting and I grew tired and weary. I had pushed myself to the limit, I had given everything I had, and I didn't have much left to give. After five and a half long months, the day came for final inspection and I could not believe my ears when he said we could move in. It was just before Thanksgiving and I was giving thanks that it was over. We were less than one month away from the expected arrival of our new son, Luke. We had just enough time to get moved in.

We moved in and Kari instantly lit up like a Christmas tree. She loved that house so much. Building the house ourselves allowed us financially, to build it just like we wanted. It was a four bedroom house and including the garage, it was 2700 square feet. Like our house in Williamsport, it had the open floor plan with vaulted ceilings but I added some custom crown molding, an entry way with granite tile and a column supporting a the entry way wall, and other special touches throughout the house. She told everyone she knew about how great of a job I did. She was so proud of me and so proud of what we had accomplished. I loved the house too but it wasn't long before I started getting the itch again for more land. As the months went by, I started thinking more and more about my dream and I started to get restless. I felt like a young child being told to sit still and be quite in church. I felt like a caged animal. I wanted more.

I was sitting at the computer one day looking at land for sale, like I routinely did, when I came across something special. It was a listing for a house sitting on 32 acres of woods for sale. It fit all my criteria I was searching for, the most important of which, my wife Kari and I could afford it. In the back of my mind, I figured I was wasting my time. It was more my dream than Kari's to own a large piece of land. We had just spent five months of our lives building our new house and we had just relocated yet again. We were just getting settled. We were just getting to know people. I instantly printed the property out and I just couldn't wait to show her. I didn't know it at the time, but this very seemingly small event would forever change my life.

When Kari got home from work that day I quickly grabbed the paper hot off the printer, gave her a gigantic smile, and handed it to her. While she glanced at the paper, I tried to sell it the best I could. "This is the perfect time to relocate," I said. "Lauren will be starting first grade next year and it would be best if we moved now before she started a new school and this is exactly what we have been looking for and you can't beat that price. Luke is only one. He doesn't even know anybody here yet." As you can expect, she was just filled with jubilation at the notion of picking up her life and moving out of her new house that she loved……..yeah right. She wasn't cold or cruel in any way, but as she handed the paper back to me, she let me know she didn't care for the idea of leaving our house that she loved. I hadn't set my expectations too high, so although I was a bit disappointed, I knew the reality of the situation. I respected and loved Kari more than anything. I certainly wasn't going to force her to do something she didn't want to do. I put my dream on hold and the paper containing the property got lost in a stack of papers somewhere and life went on. Days turned into weeks. Weeks turned into months. Nothing was said and I didn't bring it up.

I was working night shift at this time and my schedule was 6pm to 6am. My typical routine was to come home from work, chat with my wife for a few minutes, and then fall into my soft and cozy bed. Upon arising on an otherwise typical morning, Kari had a glow and an enthusiasm about her when I stumbled into the overwhelmingly bright living room, still rubbing my eyes from just waking up. "Guess what I did today," she said. "I called those people about that property. Do you want to go look at it?" I was instantly filled with incredible joy from this mind blowing news. I knew exactly what property she was talking about. Could this really be happening? Am I dreaming? All kinds of thoughts were racing through my mind but to be honest, the greatest feeling I felt at that moment was love. A deep love for my wife, not because of what she was possibly allowing me to get, but because of the love she was showing me by sacrificing her new house for my dream.

I was instantly filled with all kinds of questions. I wanted to know all the details about the phone call. "Did you get directions? When can we go see it? So it's still for sale?" The next thrilling hour was spent planning our trip as I transformed our living room into a dance floor, dancing around with jubilation.

First on our agenda was to figure out where Greencastle was located. Neither one of us had ever stepped foot in Greencastle and we knew nothing about it. We pulled out the map, charted the course and made plans to make the long anticipated trip. Kari called the property owners back to set up a day and time for us to see their home. The following Saturday morning, after awaking with overflowing emotion and extra pep in my step, we made the trip.

The drive there was filled with anticipation and excitement. I could even sense a liveliness and zestfulness in Kari about this trip that I hadn't noticed before. It was all still a dream at this point because of all the uncertainties, but I couldn't help but be overflowing with joy. After all, this was a dream that I had since I was a little boy. Ever since I can remember, I would tell friends that someday I would own a large wooded property. I couldn't help but think about that on the way. Someday may be coming very soon.

We arrived at the North side of Greencastle after about an hour trip. There was nothing special about the landscape on the way there. It was mostly farm fields filled with corn and soybeans, and the ground was flat and dull, so I was expecting the same thing when we arrived. As we drove through town, Kari and I starting talking about everything that we saw and we both felt it seemed like a nice place.

It took us about five minutes to reach the road that the house sat on. The road was just one block from the downtown square. The square was made up of many old tall buildings which housed several small businesses, a bank, and county offices. It was small town living that we were used to. As we discussed the possibilities of living in this new town, I think we both had a sense that this might be a great place to live. It just felt like home.

As we approached West Walnut Street, I turned on the right turn signal, and all that remained between us and the property was seven miles of open road. My stomach started feeling the flutter of tiny butterflies from all the anticipation, excitement, and anxiety. It was a funny feeling of being excited and nervous at the same time. All the momentum and build up to this moment, after years and years of dreaming, and all the hard work that I had done to be in the position to purchase such a property, was becoming almost paralyzing to me.

It was amazing how the landscape changed as we left town and headed west. The flat farm fields were replaced with rolling hills, flowing creeks, wooded ravines, and wildflowers everywhere you looked. My eyes must have been as wide as they have ever been trying to take in all the splendor and beauty that God had created. I found myself driving at a snail's pace to take it all in. It was a cloudy and dreary day but I didn't notice. I just saw dreams, possibilities, and tranquility. Kari and I smiled the whole way.

We finally came to the part in the road that split into two directions. Our written directions said that this is where the property was supposed to be. Kari spotted the blue house sitting back off the road a couple hundred feet, nestled amongst the trees. She shouted, "That's it, that's it!!" We then crossed a county bridge over a small creek and turned into the crushed stone driveway. The drive was a long one, around 250 feet or so. It split an open field into two pieces and I guessed it to be around an acre, with close to half an acre on each side of the drive. The slow ride up the drive was surreal as I took in the beauty of all that I saw. The field was full of color with tall green grasses and blue and yellow wild flowers. As we got within one hundred feet of the house, there was another creek to cross. It was a crystal clear stream, approximately twelve feet across, with a depth of one foot. To say I wasn't a bit nervous to cross this creek would be a lie. The bridge was constructed of weathered wood and consisted of eight foot 4x4's lying on end with small one inch gaps between each one where you could see the creek below. Below the 4x4's I could see two steel I beams, that were set in concrete slabs on each side of the creek bank, that supported the wooden structure. I centered our white minivan's tires over the steel I beams the best I could, and quickly drove across. My stomach was already a mess from the excitement of the day, so I felt relieved getting across the wooden bridge and pulling up to the house and parking.

We knocked on the gray steel door, and after a quick meet and greet with the owners, we toured the house. The house was originally a two room dirt floor log cabin built in the 1970's by a local college professor, but it had undergone major renovation four or five years earlier. Not only did they add a room addition to the existing cabin, they also added a second story over the entire structure. As it stood now, it was a fairly large house containing 2200 square feet, with four bedrooms, the amount Kari and I both wanted. Parts of the house were still in need of some repairs but we both saw possibilities. I found my listening skills to be suffering greatly as we were wrapping up the tour. I was extremely anxious to go outside so when the owners asked if we wanted to walk the property, I thought to myself, are you kidding me? I had waited my whole life for this day. We quickly went outside and started the hike that exceeded even my dreams expectations.

I picked up my rapidly growing one year old son Luke, and Kari held Lauren's small hand as we started the adventure into the great unknown. It was at this point I realized just how much that Luke had taken after me with his love for food as he clearly had gained two pounds since yesterday. I knew this hike would be quite the workout for me and knew only the pure will to make my dream become reality, could propel me to finish it.

As a child I remember my parents taking me to Turkey Run State park located in Parke County in West Central Indiana. I remember how beautiful it was with large sandstone rocks, large ravines, deep canyons, and clear streams. I suppose Turkey Run along with a few other State parks my parents took us to, kindled the fire in me that has never gone out. This fire in me became my dream to own a woods and here I was entering a woods that could very well become my own.

As we started the hike, we were in no way ready for what we were about to see. Our jaws dropped to the ground. Our eyes were wide open. To own your own woods is one thing but to own a place with so much beauty and character is quite another. The property looked like a mini version of turkey run. It had large ravines with fresh flowing springs with mini waterfalls over limestone moss covered rocks. It had deep canyons that you had to see to believe. It had large limestone rock formations that were so large, I could stand under them. The woods abounded with naturally growing ferns, lily of the valley, jack of the pulpits, blackberry briars, and wild flowers everywhere you looked. There was a great variety of tree species: Oak, walnut, poplar, sycamore, sassafras, maple, and birch trees. On the back South West corner of the property there was a steep cliff that overlooked one of two creeks that bordered the property. The creek must have been some 200-300 feet below. The view was breathtaking.

We continued on from the creek which was on the west end of the property and hiked east. We crossed a small ravine and because of the thick brush, somehow Kari and I got separated. As I got my bearings and was trying to figure out where she might have gone, I hear Kari yelling through the woods. "Jason!! Jason get over here!" I hurried through the thick brush in the direction of where I heard her voice. I was a bit concerned that something might have happened or someone might have gotten hurt. Much to my amusement, I find her on the side of a steep ravine, hanging on for dear life, pointing to a wild ginseng plant. With much enthusiasm in her voice she said, "There is ginseng here, look at this! It is everywhere!" I was thinking to myself that God may have just answered my prayers by placing something so very irresistible to my wife, on this property but I tried not to make a big deal out of it. I didn't want to press my luck and be overbearing. I wanted this more than anything but I knew if it was meant to be, then it would happen.

With Kari now yielding a smile that would not let up the rest of the hike, we made our way through the woods to the South East corner of the property, following the wide freshly mowed trail; we came to another large canyon. Standing at the top of this canyon yielded a picture perfect view below of a fresh flowing spring and limestone rocks. We followed the edge of this canyon down to the bottom and eventually made our way out to an open field. The field was around 150 feet wide by 500 feet long. It was grown up with white, blue, and yellow, wildflowers and was full of song birds and beautiful butterflies. We walked across the field and came to the front of the property which was bordered by the second creek. The creek was shallow, an average depth of one foot or so, crystal clear, and gently flowing. It had many ripples and waves from the water flowing over rocks in the creek bed. The sound of the water rushing over the rocks was relaxing and serene.

We followed the creek back toward the house, walking through the open field. It took us around five minutes to make the hike back. We had yet to see where the creeks joined in front of the house so we decided to head there. The creeks came together only a few hundred feet away from the house. Both creeks were shallow streams with lots of ripples, stones, waves, and bubbling water. As we approached the water we noticed one side of the creek bank was nothing but beautiful, white, powdery sand.

Kari and I told the owners we needed to talk a few minutes so we walked along the creek to create some distance between us. Our conversation was quick and to the point. There was really no discussion. We both knew what we had to do. We had to call our realtor when we got home and put our house on the market. After our discussion, we walked back over to the owners. We told them emphatically, we wanted the place. We decided on a price and we let them know that we would be putting our house up for sale as soon as possible. I took one last quick look around in the front yard. I wanted a moment to think. I was trying to let all the sights, all the excitement, all that I had just experienced, sink in. It wasn't long before I was snapped back into reality with my exhausted children letting me know they were tired and ready to go, so we loaded Luke and Lauren into the van. In the brief moment it took to buckle the kids in their car seats, so many thoughts raced through my mind. I knew how much Kari loved our new house in Lafayette. I knew to move wouldn't be easy for her. Even though it was Kari's idea to look at the house on that day, I still had my doubts. Those doubts were quickly erased on the ride home.

Words cannot express the high felt on that ride home. If there was something above cloud nine, we were there. The van was filled with smiles, laughter, dreams, and possibilities. We started working on our plans to remodel the house. We started talking about everything we wanted to do outside. We discussed the benefits of raising our children in a place with so much room to run and so many places to explore. The next chapter in our lives seemed it was about to begin, and we couldn't help but be optimistic that it was going to be, by far, the best one yet. It was during this time that I realized my dream became Kari's dream.

The next few months were filled with highs and lows as we were going through the selling process. Every time the phone would ring, our hearts would race hoping it was the realtor calling. Many prospective buyers came to look at our house and many times we thought this is the one. One particular young man seemed really interested at first. He made a low ball offer; we countered a bit, and never heard anything again. As the days went by without hearing anything, our disappointment grew to the point of frustration. We started to feel desperate.

In the time we had the house for sale, we made three trips back to the dream property most of which was spent hiking the beautiful landscape, talking about our dreams. Try as we may, we just couldn't stay away. It was our third trip there and after hiking through the woods and making more plans about our future, we had a revelation. We needed to call our realtor and make a counter offer with the young man that had made an offer before. We had no idea if he had bought a house yet but I don't think either of us could take not being able to get the property. It was consuming our every thought, and it is all we talked about. While still hiking in the woods at our dream property, we put the call in to the realtor while standing between a couple poplar trees. The very next day, while patiently waiting at home, we got a call back. The realtor explained to us the young man had accepted the offer and it was just a matter of him getting his inspections done and getting a closing date. As I hung up the phone, I could not control my emotions. I took a deep breath and then, at the top of my lungs, did my best impersonation of Bo Duke's Yeeeeeeee Haaaaaaaw!! I'm not sure if it's true, but they say you could hear it all the way in Lafayette, some seven miles away.

The next several hours were filled with tears, with laughter, and with permanently molded smiles. We hugged, we kissed, and we jumped up and down. We were overrun with joy as 'the day' had come. The rollercoaster of the past several weeks was coming to an end. My dream that I had wanted my entire life and that Kari and I had worked so hard for, for so many years, was about to come true. At this moment it hit me. The dream was no longer a thought, a vision, or a fantasy. It was real. It had come true. We were living the dream.

The weeks that followed were an exciting and busy time for us. We had so much to do and so little time to do it. Inspections, packing, planning, we were so busy. We somehow found time to make one last trip to the property. When we arrived, the property owner Mike was mowing the main trail in the woods with their tractor. It was a 1960's open cab, Massey Fergusson 50 farm tractor. It was a large tractor with back tires that came up to my shoulders. It had a bucket on the front for moving dirt and rocks, and it also had a beat up bush hog on the back for mowing. It was red and was weathered with rust from years of use. It wasn't pretty but it seemed to work quite well. After some discussion, Kari and I arrived at the decision to purchase the tractor with the house. We knew nothing about tractors, nor had we ever driven one, as we had both been raised in the city. We knew though, with buying 32 acres, we would need it to care for the place. We talked with Mike for a bit longer, went for a hike in the woods, and then headed back home.

Isaiah 41:13
For I am the LORD, your God, who takes
hold of your right hand and says to you, Do
not fear; I will help you.
(NIV)

CHAPTER 2

THE MOVE

After years and years of anticipation, the day was here. May 26th, 2006. Today was the day we were embarking on yet another new adventure……..the adventure of all adventures. This was a day like no other we had experienced. This day was special. As exciting as this day was, there was a level of anxiety because there were so many unknowns, so many uncertainties. It was honestly kind of a scary time. We didn't have any family or friends in Greencastle. We didn't have a church there. Kari had always worked and she did not have a job yet and we knew money would be tight until she found something. We would have to rely on our relationship and friendship with each other to get us through. We would have to rely on God to provide.

When we first got it confirmed from our realtor, move day seemed so far away but our constant busyness had the time flying by. Weeks turned into days, and days turned into now. Many trips had already been made to Greencastle in the past month to fill a storage unit just south of town, so the house and garage were already partially emptied. We wanted to be sure we could fit the rest of our belongings that were left in the house, into the moving truck so we wouldn't have to make another trip.

We started move day by running into Lafayette and renting a 24' U-Haul moving truck. We wanted to be at the rental store to pick up the truck when they opened at 8am, as this was to be a very busy day. When we got home with the truck, we loaded and packed, and packed and loaded, until every single item in the house had been removed. We kept a close eye on the clock as we had to be in Greencastle to close on the new property at 1pm, and 1pm was just a few short hours away. After loading was complete, with fatigued legs and achy backs, we made one final check of the house to be sure nothing was left. We stopped and reminisced as we went into each room.

It had only been a little over a year ago that we brought little Luke home to his freshly finished room and the house was full of his baby memories. Lauren loved her room, loved the yard, and had often played with the neighbor girl next door. We had put so much work and sweat into the house to make it just like we wanted. Even though we were full of anticipation for what awaited us in Greencastle, it was not easy to say goodbye. I closed and locked the heavy oak front door and another chapter in our life, the most anticipated chapter in our life, had begun.

We arrived in Greencastle just in time to make our 1pm appointment. I was lucky enough to find enough empty parking spaces together to park that big truck downtown on the square as Kari parked the van around the corner. I met up with Kari and the kids out in front of the old brick building. It was really hard to hold back our overflowing emotions so there was no use trying. Kari and I both walked into the building smiling from ear to ear and a bit giddy. As soon as we opened the large door, we were greeted inside by a pleasant middle aged woman, and then taken to a room in the back of the building, with a long, dark, wooden table. The sellers had already arrived and were seated at the table across from where we were to sit down. We sat Luke on the floor still strapped in his car seat, sat Lauren down and found her some paper to draw on, and then we began the carpal tunnel producing process.

Each time I signed my name I knew I was one step closer to paradise. My mind started drifting to the rolling hills, flowing streams, and colorful wildflowers when I was quickly snapped back into reality when a wretched stench filled the air of the title company. The timing could not have been worse when Luke unexpectedly, decided it was time to fill his size 2T pants. The signing of this loan was one of, if not the most important document signings in recent history and to have it interrupted with an incredible odor of such magnitude, somehow seemed demeaning. Kari quickly scrambled to dispatch my young son's donation and then we proceeded to finish up with the paperwork. With our noses plugged and the last signature in place, we loaded back into our vehicles and made the eight minute drive to home.

The drive to our new home was a dangerous one. Driving that curvy and hilly road in a car is one thing. Driving that road with a big loaded down truck while you are filled with an overwhelming sense of joy is quite another. I somehow managed to hold back my emotions and excitement enough to keep the oversized truck on the road and I arrived safely at my destination.

As I pulled up the drive toward the house, I started getting a funny feeling in my stomach and no, this time it was not gas pain. I had a tough decision to make. Could this large truck make it across the wooden bridge? At the closing, I had talked to the sellers about it and they said it would probably be OK. Probably did not settle with me well as that left a chance for bad things to happen.

It is estimated that a fully loaded 24' U-Haul weighs approximately 18,000 pounds or 9 tons. The thought of unloading all of our belongings and carrying them the 100+ feet to the door pretty much convinced me to give it a shot. Then I started having doubts. What is the worst that can happen? The bridge could collapse and the 18,000 pounds, with me in it, would drop around 12-15 feet, into a shallow stream and I would be killed instantly. With the thought of my dream quickly turning into a nightmare, I started getting pretty nervous. After studying the construction of the bridge, it was decided if the tires of the vehicle stayed right above the steel 'I' beams under the wood construction; I would be ok, well maybe. I lined up the tires the best I could, said a quick prayer to the good Lord, and held my breath as I punched the gas pedal. The trip across took no longer than four or five seconds but seemed like four or five minutes. During the short trip, in my mind I think I played 12 different outcomes of crossing the bridge as I drove across, and all of them ended in a painful death. I was drenched with sweat and relieved beyond words, when the back wheels cleared the bridge and rolled onto the rocks of the solid driveway. We were home.

As we unloaded the jam packed truck, the reality that my dream had come true started sinking in. I had to pinch myself several times, and although I was living my dream, I was not dreaming. This was real. Each time Kari and I walked out of the house to get another item from the truck, we found ourselves staring, daydreaming, and wandering about aimlessly. I suddenly diagnosed myself with ADD although I had never experienced those symptoms before. It literally took twice as long as what it should have, or could have taken, but this day wasn't about how efficient we could be or fast we could move. We took in the moment and enjoyed it so very much.

I had decided to take a week off work so we could get settled into our new house. I knew we had a lot of work to get done and I wanted to get started right away. That week was insanely busy as we were working feverishly from awakening until bedtime. Of course, with that busyness came the necessity to eat out a lot. We had made a considerable amount of money selling our house in Lafayette and we put aside a portion of that money to blow. We used this blow money to finance our eating on the run. Those first few weeks, we pretty much ate out every meal. It became so regular that my one year old son Luke knew it was time to eat when he saw a drive up ordering sign. Every time we pulled up to order he would start clapping his hands to show his gratitude. Even though we knew it was coming, Kari and I would laugh every time.

We spent most of our time at the house, working on it. We gave the entire inside of the house a makeover. We painted every room. We hung new interior doors upstairs. We installed new trim upstairs and new light fixtures throughout the house. We tore out a couple small walls upstairs to make some rooms bigger. We worked tirelessly. We had so much we wanted to do and we wanted it all done yesterday. We had plans for a family get-together on Father's day and there was a lot we wanted to have done before then.

As Fathers day drew closer, we started working outside more and more. The grass and weeds had been neglected as we worked like crazy to get the inside done and we wanted the outside to look nice for our get together. Working outside in the beautiful sunny summer weather, was a nice escape from being cooped up inside every day and it allowed us enjoy the property a bit more. We fired up that old Massey Ferguson tractor and we mowed the front field, the back field, and even our front yard. All together it was a good 3-4 acres so it was a lot to mow. Of course Kari had to get her turn on the tractor. When it came to machinery, she wasn't afraid of anything and if it had a steering wheel, she wanted to drive. She was a bit of a tomboy as she had always loved to hang out with her dad and watch him work on cars when she was growing up.

There was much anticipation for Father's day. We were so very proud of our new home and we wanted to share it with our family. The day ended up being cloudy with some rain but there was nothing that could put a damper on our elation to show our family our new homestead. I cooked juicy hamburgers and spicy chicken on our new grill we had just purchased, we took four wheeler rides on the trails in the woods, we played horseshoes, and we even had photo time with people taking turns posing on that old red tractor. Our family seemed to love the place as much as we did and we enjoyed every minute of the day.

After the Fathers day festivities were over and the last person had left, Kari and I talked about the day as we cleaned up. We were filled with pride and filled with joy. It was great to share our dream with the whole family and they seemed to share our excitement for the place. We were feeling really good about how the house was coming along and we couldn't wait to finish it up.

With the bright sun and the sounds of songbirds coming through our open bedroom windows, we awoke the next day early and got right back to work. About three weeks after the move, I started to get run down and frustrated. I was so tired from the nonstop work. I felt I was teetering on the edge of sanity. How could this be? This was not at all how I envisioned my dream. This all kind of hit me one evening as I was working in Luke's bedroom. Kari entered the room and suggested what I should work on next, when I finished up in the bedroom. I had, had all I could stand and I knew things needed to change so with a bit of emotion I said, "We need to slow down! Life is too short! Let's enjoy this place a little bit. We have been here three weeks and have hardly had any fun time. I want to go into the woods. I want to relax a bit. This work will be here tomorrow. There is no hurry." Kari could not contest what I had said and she agreed we would slow down. After I finished my project, the whole family went for a hike in the woods.

That next week was much more enjoyable. We still got a lot of work done but now we were scheduling in regular breaks from the work. Every evening around supper time, we would stop working and do something fun before dark. These breaks made the work much more tolerable and allowed us to enjoy ourselves and our new home.

Several evenings after we finished our work, we went for short, relaxing hikes. On many occasions we would spot deer and watch them from a distance as they fed in a nearby farm field. We also waded our two creeks all the way to the ends of our property, taking in all the beauty of the place. Several places in the creek had solid rock bottoms and many places had the same white sand shorelines as we had in front of the house. The water was crystal clear and many small creek chub and an occasional striped snake swam by us during our trips.

I recall one evening in particular in the fourth week of our move that I will never forget. Kari and I were swinging in our new wooden swing I had just put together. The swing hung right next to the bubbling creek with the sandy beach shoreline in front of the house. The sun was shining, the birds were singing, and the creek was making a relaxing sound as the water rushed over the small rocks. Kari had a big smile on her face when she said, "I think I am going to like it here." These words meant so much to me. At that moment I knew we had absolutely found the right place. Kari had always struggled with moving away from home. Even in Lafayette, where she loved the house, she never felt at home. Never had she been so optimistic about her future. I knew I was going to love it in Greencastle but I would never truly be happy if I knew Kari wasn't. I knew that from our experience in Williamsport. If there was any doubt left in my mind about this being just my dream, it was erased. Kari was having fun. Kari was loving it.

The few free hours I had the next day, were spent outside. I had to go to work that night so Kari and I were just hanging out, spending some time together. As we walked across the front yard on that beautiful sunny day, Kari's attention was drawn to a couple small tree stumps, approximately 20 inches in diameter that were right in the middle of the yard. Had they been cut off at the ground it wouldn't have really been an issue, but these were a couple feet tall. I assured her that I could get them dug up and cut out in the next day or two. We soon headed back in the house as I had to leave for work soon. This was to be my last night at work before having three days off.

As I was getting ready for work that evening, I decided I was going to drive the truck in to work and stop off at our storage unit in Lafayette in the morning. When we put the house for sale, we had moved some of our stuff to the storage unit so that there would be less clutter in the house. I wanted to get everything out of there as quickly as I could, so we wouldn't have to pay another months' rent.

That night while I was working, Kari was going to drive the van to the home improvement store and pick up a new shower for our bathroom as this was the next project on my list. When I was about to leave, Kari asked me what else she should do that evening, like she usually did on a

Friday night when I had to work. It just so happened that a store was having an Indianapolis Colts rally that evening in the town she was headed to, and we were both huge Colts fans. I suggested she check that out while she was there. As I walked out the door to leave, I paused for a brief moment. What was I doing, I thought to myself? Here we both were, so caught up making things just right at the house that we were neglecting the very foundation of the home, our relationship. It seemed we both realized that at that very moment. Kari and I stood at the door and looked into each other's eyes and kissed. It was a special moment and seemed to be an awakening for us both.

My night at work was slow. The process that I operated lasted for several days. Some days you were extremely busy. Some days you were extremely bored. This night was the latter. It was around 9pm when the phone rang inside the office where I was monitoring things. Kari was calling after just leaving the Colt's rally. She had, had a great night and she was eager to tell me all about it. After she had picked up the glass shower for our bathroom, she and the kids headed down to the rally. She was thrilled to tell me she got to meet several Colts' players and Lauren got to meet some of their cheerleaders. I was a bit jealous that I wasn't able to be there, but I was happy they had fun.

We must have talked for an hour or so on the phone that night. It was so refreshing to just talk. Our busyness over the last several months had really caused a strain on the family and we just hadn't been communicating enough. It seemed this conversation was a continuance from what had happened on our front porch that night, and I thoroughly enjoyed every minute of it. We had learned from our mistakes and we were ready to slow down and enjoy our time together.

As the night shift came to a close, I started regretting my decision to stop off at the storage unit. The building was about 20 minutes out of the way and this would mean my drive home would be around an hour and a half instead of just over one hour. I was tired and I just wanted to get home but being who I am, I had to get it done.

After work I made the short trip to the storage unit and loaded up the truck the best I could but it unfortunately it would still take one more trip to empty it. It was a bright sunny morning and I found it hard to stay awake on the drive home. I tried everything I could think of to stay awake. I turned the radio up. I rolled the windows down to get air blowing on my face. I even shook my head from side to side, all to no avail. I was so grateful when I finally made it to our road. As I was driving down my road that morning, I was awoken with deer crossing the road right in front of my truck. It brought a smile to my face to see wildlife all around and it made me realize just how lucky I was to have finally found my place. After seeing the deer, it was a bit easier to stay awake the last few miles and I knew my destination was within reach. I could soon crawl into my inviting bed.

When I pulled in the drive I thought for a second that I could unload the truck right then but that thought quickly faded. It was nearly 8am and I would be getting up soon anyway, as this was my normal routine on my first day off from work. I quickly showered and headed to the bedroom. Everyone was still in bed when my tired, heavy, legs made their way up the stairs. Kari was lying there in bed awake when I walked into the room. I told her how tired I had been all night and how hard it was to stay awake on the drive home. She lovingly asked why I went to the storage unit if I was so tired. She told me I was crazy when I told her it needed to get done. I concurred with her and without wasting another second; I quickly climbed into my nice, cozy, soft, bed. I set the alarm clock for 11:45am; we talked for a minute and then I started drifting off. I was in a state of semi consciousness, and was fading fast, when she was getting out of bed. She gave me a kiss and we exchanged I love you's, and then I was out.

2 CORINTHIANS 5:7

WE LIVE BY FAITH, NOT BY SIGHT. (NIV)

Chapter 3

THE DAY

I woke up suddenly to the sound of Lauren screaming frantically, "Daddy, Daddy, come quick. It's a hurricane, it's a hurricane! The tractor is on top of Mommy!!" I tried my best to wake up and try to understand what was going on. My stomach dropped as I knew something was wrong but my level of alertness made it hard for me to properly access the situation. Again, Lauren yelled out, "It's a hurricane, it's a hurricane!" Finally my thoughts started coming together as I threw off my covers and jumped out of bed. I looked over at Lauren and saw a scared and worried little child. Her face was pale in complexion and covered with fear. Upon seeing her reaction to whatever was going on outside, I felt an incredible tightening of my chest and my stomach starting twisting and turning like nothing I had ever experienced. My mind raced. My heart raced to the point of pain. I raced down the stairs as fast as I could go and ran out of the front door with no shoes and no shirt.

As soon as I opened the front door I saw the old tractor in the front yard, upside down. At that moment, my world stopped. I could not hear a thing other than my pounding heart that continued to go at an incredible pace. I ran toward my wife as fast as I could possibly go, but it seemed like I was standing still. As I made my way to the tractor, I didn't want to believe what had happened. In the short time it took to get to her, so many thoughts ran through my mind. She might be hurt, but not badly. Surely she is just stuck and can't get out. I will be able to help her when I get over there, and she will be fine. I just knew that everything was going to be ok. My thoughts of positivity changed quickly when I dove onto the ground near the tractor. There was my beautiful wife and best friend, right before my eyes, unconscious and unresponsive. I could tell she was hurt but I still wasn't sure exactly how bad. There was very little blood to be seen and for the most part, she was untouched from the heavy tractors weight. I noticed the stiff hydraulic lines of the tractor were pressing against her neck, so I lifted and pulled with all my might, but I couldn't move them. I yelled her name again and again and got no response. I picked up her motionless, warm arm and tried to find a pulse, searching for some kind of hope, but I couldn't find any. At this point I started losing my mental focus. I couldn't think clearly. I tried frantically to figure out what to do, but my mind was not working. I finally gathered my thoughts enough to run into the house and call 911.

The call to 911 was a frantic mess. It was hard for me to speak. I tried to tell the operator my address but my speech was slurred and my words were running together. I had so much adrenaline running through my veins that I was shaking uncontrollably. It made holding onto the phone and talking extremely difficult. After the attentive operator got my information and tried the best they could to calm me down under the circumstances, I hung up the phone, grabbed the keys to the four wheeler, and ran out the door. I rode that thing faster than I had ever ridden it, to the neighbors across the street.

My neighbor owned heavy machinery so I thought they may be able to help. As soon as I pulled into their drive I saw a group of guys standing outside at their trucks, talking. I yelled as loud as I could, "The tractor is on my wife, the tractor is on my wife!!" They all quickly scrambled and one of them ran to a backhoe and climbed in, as I sped down their gravel drive toward home. When I got home, I jumped off the four wheeler and ran as fast as I could to my wife. In my mind I was hoping that somehow things would be different when I got to her this time, that maybe the first time I didn't see things right. Maybe I was too tired and confused to see things clearly. But when I reached her, everything was the same. Again I pulled on those hydraulic lines with all my might, and again, they just wouldn't budge. There was nothing I could do. I waited there next to my motionless wife feeling so helpless and hopeless. My stomach hurt. My mind hurt. My heart hurt.

The men from across the road made their way up the drive and across the yard to the accident scene. After one of the men made a quick examination of Kari, they quickly realized what I already knew. With a sad and distant look on his face, the man that reached down to feel for a pulse shook his head no and said, "She is gone." Again, everything went silent. I couldn't hear any cars going by. I heard no birds singing. It was as if the world just stopped. My world had just stopped. The silence was broken when the men told me there was nothing they could do. I didn't scream. I didn't cry. I just stood there emotionless. I instantly felt a numb, emptiness inside of me and mentally I just went away.

I turned to walk to the house and saw frightened little Lauren was standing there, not 100 feet from where the tractor set. Through all the madness and sadness, I had forgotten all about her. How scared and confused she must have been standing there all alone watching things unfold. I grabbed her little hand and told her to come with me. Without saying a word, we slowly walked over to the front porch, went inside, and shut the front door.

Immediately after I shut the door Lauren started screaming hysterically. "Who is going to take me to school now? Who is going to fix my hair? Who is going to watch me when you are at work?" The horrific look of fear on her face tugged at my emotions and drained me of what little energy I had left. Even at the age of six years old, she knew when we shut that door that her mom was gone and never coming back. I was heartbroken. I was devastated. How could I possibly be a rock for my frightened and fragile little girl? At this moment, I felt the presence of God with me. I had no strength of my own as it was hard for me to even stand, but I comforted Lauren and told her everything would be just fine. I told her we had each other and we had God. With tears running down my face, we held hands and prayed together right there in the kitchen. This gave us both a sense of peace. Lauren stopped crying and screaming and we walked together to the living room.

When we walked in I immediately went over to the French doors that overlooked the front yard, where Kari lay, and closed the curtains. We had both seen more than we could handle and we wanted shelter from our reality. With not knowing what else to do, we both sat on the couch motionless and quiet. As we sat there for a few minutes, we could hear sirens and commotion outside, but we dare not look. I couldn't handle seeing any more. As if what I had to deal with at that moment wasn't enough, I somehow had to find the strength to make the phone calls to the family just minutes after my wife and best friend died. As I made the short walk into the kitchen for the phone, my heart ached, my mind raced, and my stomach twisted into what seemed like a thousand knots. I wanted to run. I wanted to scream. I wanted my wife back. With my legs weak and trembling, I sat down in a kitchen chair with the phone in hand. I decided to call Kari's dad, my mom, and Kari's friend Desiree. I knew these three people could relay the information to the rest of our family and friends. As expected the calls were painful, gut wrenching and filled with tears and extreme sadness, but they were also met with shock and disbelief for no one was ready for what I was about to tell them.

Kari's dad, Bill, had just talked to his daughter on the phone, just minutes earlier. As she was working outside on that bright, sunny day, she called him to tell him she was trying to remove those tree stumps with the tractor. I can only imagine the heartache and pain he must have felt as I told him what had happened. As I explained the best I could with my broken and crackling voice, he repeated over and over back to me in a voice of desperation, "I just talked to her. I just talked to her."

With all of my family at least two hours away, Desiree volunteered to come to the house. I felt comfort in knowing someone familiar would be there soon. I didn't know Desiree well but she was a friend of Kari's and I felt comfort in knowing that. She and her family lived an hour away in Lafayette, but there was no time to rest while waiting for her arrival.

There was knock after knock at the door. The fire chaplain was first to show up on our door step. I welcomed him in and we proceeded to the living room. He prayed with us and gave us comfort. I appreciated his prayers and kind words. As we were sitting on the coach talking, I started hearing Luke talking from his room upstairs. I had completely forgotten all about him. My heart instantly started hurting more at the thought of his one year old innocence. I went upstairs to his bedroom and found him standing up, holding onto to his baby bed rails, with a huge grin on his face. He had no idea what had just happened to his mom, but his life had forever been changed. My already broken heart broke again.

Many others showed up and wanted to talk to me but I felt like it was such an invasion. I didn't want to talk. I just wanted to be left alone so I could take in all that had happened. With each knock on the door, I felt more stressed and more uncomfortable. I just wanted them to go away. The most difficult visitors were from the sheriff's department. I know they were just doing their job but I was broken and had nothing to give. Every question was an insult as just the idea of some kind of foul play turned my stomach. My best friend just died and I had to answer interrogation questions. It just didn't seem right to me.

As soon as they finished their investigation, the coroner was waiting to speak with me. The coroner's job is to tell you as delicately as he can that your spouse is dead, which I guess he did quite well. There is just no good way of comforting someone in that situation. He told me that everything went well and that they didn't have any problems freeing Kari from the tractor and that she was now in the front field. I really hated hearing about the details. I didn't care where my dead wife's body lay. I just wanted them gone. I wanted them all gone.

The last knock at the door was from a volunteer fireman from the fire station just a few miles up our road. They were offering to haul the tractor away and store it for me. I thought it was a noble gesture and agreed to let them take it away. I hadn't thought about it, but I was so glad I didn't have to see that old red tractor again.

As things started settling down at the house, and the fireman drove away with the tractor, Desiree pulled into the drive. I could see a deep sense of compassion and pain in her eyes when she walked through the door and we immediately embraced with a loving hug. It felt good to have someone to share my grief with, someone that knew Kari. She did a fantastic job of taking care of the kids and cleaning up around the house. She allowed me to take in everything that had happened. She allowed me to finally breathe.

As it got closer to supper time, I walked into the kitchen and Desiree asked me if I wanted something to eat but eating was far, far from my mind. My stomach could not even handle the thought of food, let alone eating. I was running on a couple hours sleep, I was exhausted, empty, and drained. I left the kitchen and slowly made my way upstairs with heavy legs and a heavy heart and filled the tub for a bath. I lie in the bath for quite some time not moving and not really thinking but just feeling empty and numb.

That evening I escaped to our bedroom as family members started arriving. In our room I tried to stand. I tried to pace. I tried to lie down. There was no getting comfortable on this day.

There was nothing I could do. There was nowhere I could go to outrun the pain. It just was and I hated every moment of it. While alone in our room, my mind thought about all that had happened. I was so scared and so alone. In an instant, I was a single parent and solely responsible for my two children. I had always felt that Kari was the better parent than I was. It didn't seem fair that she died and I got to live. My alarm clock was set to go off 15 minutes before Lauren woke me up. A mere 20 minutes stood between life and death for my wife. Had I listened to Kari and not went to the storage unit after work, I would have been up an hour earlier and the accident never would have happened. I felt an extreme sense of guilt about making the wrong choices. So many would of, should of, could of, but that wouldn't change anything now. This is my new normal. She is gone and she is not coming back.

My bed felt like the Great Plains that night as I lie down to go to sleep. It was large, empty, and I felt isolated from the world. I felt as if I were lost in a giant forest, desperate and lonely, and wanting to find my way back home to what I knew. I wanted things to stay the same. I was extremely exhausted but my eyes were wide awake. I cried all night long. I tossed and turned trying to find rest but it wasn't happening. My mind would not shut down. It wasn't for long, but at some point during the night, I finally fell asleep.

Revelation 21:4

He will wipe every tear from their eyes.
There will be no more death or mourning or
crying or pain, for the old order of things
has passed away. **(NIV)**

CHAPTER 4

THE FUNERAL

I awoke to an unsettling feeling in my
stomach as the waves of what happened the day
before rushed over me. I wondered for a brief
moment if it had all really happened or if it was
just a bad dream. I lie in bed motionless. I had
no desire to move. I had no motivation to get out
of bed. Deep down I knew I must go on but for
what? My world as I knew it was gone. My
dreams were gone. My future seemed as though
it was over.

The days following the accident were a
blur. I was so numb I felt as if I was on auto
pilot. I just existed. Even if I wanted to, I really
didn't have time to feel much of anything. I had
so much to do and so many preparations to make

for the viewing and funeral. It's something I had never thought about before but what you have to deal with after someone you love dies is so much work. I have never been one to back down from work but when dealing with a loss of a loved one, you have no energy, you have nothing to give.

Much of those days leading up to the funeral I was surrounded with family and friends. This helped a great deal with keeping reality away, the reality that I was alone. To be honest, I didn't care for that much. I liked being surrounded by people but I also knew that I was avoiding the inevitable. So, as hard as it was, whenever I could, I would get away and do things alone.

I contacted my employer and they were gracious in giving me time off work. They told me to take us much time as I needed and to not come back until I was ready. Not only would I have the time off, I would also be paid while I wasn't there. It was a major blessing for us. I was also to interview with my current employer for a new position at work just two days after Kari died. They decided to move the interview back four weeks to give me a chance to mourn. Kari and I were so looking forward to the opportunity for the new position. It was a job that also meant I would be on day shift, something that Kari had wanted for a long time.

Even though Kari had always wanted me to, I have never been one to dress up. I am a jeans and t shirt kind of guy and I really didn't have anything to wear for the viewing, so I decided I needed to go shopping. My mom asked if I wanted someone to go with me but I wanted to go alone. I knew it was going to be hard but felt it was for the best. I needed to be able to think by myself. I needed an opportunity to cry.

On the drive to the mall I poured my heart out to God through praise music. I was really identifying with Jeremy Camp's music. He had been my favorite artist for several years and because of his past loss of a wife, I felt a closeness and connection when I listened to his words. He sang about walking by faith, and still believing even though he didn't understand why things happened the way they did. His songs held me together and gave me strength.

When I pulled the car into the mall parking lot, I received a phone call from a man that worked at the newspaper in Anderson, a town not far from where Kari and I both grew up. He had heard of the tragedy and he wanted to do a story on Kari. I found it very odd that he wanted to do it but felt a great sense of pride and excitement. I answered his questions and gave him permission to print the story.

The walk to the doors of the store was a slow one. My stomach was in knots and I was feeling a bit dizzy and light headed. It was the first time I had been to the store since Kari's death. I felt so alone. I felt like a scared child. After entering the store, I found my way to the men's section and after looking for awhile, found a suit jacket that I liked. I felt as if that were the easy part as I have a bit of color blindness and finding a tie to match would be more difficult. As I was looking, I started getting down and a wave of loneness rushed over me. At that moment, a young woman walked past and I reached out to her for help. I was never one to ask help for anything, so doing this was completely out of character. I told her about the accident and showed her some family pictures in my wallet. In an instant, I could see her heart break. She stopped what she was doing and immediately began to help. As she was looking through the ties, I felt tears welling up in my eyes. I was so fragile, that the thought of someone taking their time to help me was overwhelming. She must have been with me five minutes or so until we found something that I liked. She didn't really say much but I could tell by her nervousness, facial expressions and gestures that she was really moved. I was so thankful for her that day. She didn't do all that much but she meant so much to me.

I had decided early on that the funeral was going to be a positive, uplifting service. I knew Kari was in heaven, a place she often wondered about. I wanted to celebrate where she had gone and what she was experiencing. I wanted to praise God for giving us the opportunity to share in his riches. I wanted other people to see, no matter what happens, no matter the circumstances, we can still praise him. I spent several hours of the next few days planning for the funeral. I had to pick out worship music, pictures of Kari, and bible verses. I also wrote a message to be shared at the funeral. In the letter, I shared some of Kari's personal life that most other people didn't get to see. All of these preparations were a lot of work but it kept me going. Having something to keep my mind on kept some of the pain away. It gave me purpose.

I was to meet Kari's dad Bill, and sister Holly, at the funeral home to make arrangements so my mom watched the kids. The meeting at the funeral home was surreal. As the representative from the funeral home was talking, my mind started wandering. I was sitting there thinking, a few days ago I am a married man, and today I am picking out my wife's casket. It is really hard to wrap your head around that thought. I hated every minute of it. I wanted it over.

Immediately after leaving the funeral home, we went to the city cemetery to buy a burial plot. I was told by the old man working there, they had two plots side by side, but I knew right away that I didn't want to commit to that. I knew my life wasn't over and I didn't know where life would take me. After writing a large check for a hole in the ground, I quickly began to realize that this was going to be a very expensive couple days. I hated to think about money at a time like this, but I couldn't help but think about how much it was going to cost. It began to weigh on me heavily and added to my mountain of stress.

After leaving the cemetery, I stopped in at my parent's house that sits just south of town. After talking with them for a while, my mom volunteered to keep the kids for me and I drove home alone. All that I had taken in the last few days hit me as I drove alone in the car. Like a torrential downpour of rain, I cried uncontrollably for the entire two hour car ride home. I cried out to God to take the pain away.

As if I hadn't already dealt with enough that day, when I got home I went through Kari's clothes. I had to pick out what she would wear for the last time. How do you do that? I cried at just the thought. As I moved the hangers across the rack in the closet, my mind saw Kari wearing every outfit. Memories and tears started flowing together. I found Kari's favorite blue jacket and reached into the pockets. There in her left pocket, I found a receipt from Sam's Club, her favorite store that she visited the night I talked to her on the phone from work. It was her last trip to Sam's. It was her last night on earth a mere 15 hours before she would die. I fell to the closet floor on my knees, holding her soft jacket against my face, using it to soak up my tears.

The next day I received a phone call from the coroner that I had to sit down to take in. He was calling to let me know the results of the autopsy. It was news I didn't want to hear. They ruled the official cause of death, asphyxiation. Through the years, Kari and I had talked about the worst kinds of death and drowning was at the top of the list. Unable to get a breath, knowing you were going to die. We both thought it would be the worst way to go. When the coroner gave me the news, it was extremely hard for me to take in. He tried to sugar coat it the best he could, but I knew what it meant. Kari lie on the ground, pinned beneath the tractor, knowing she was going to die. She had time to think about it. This news caused me so much hurt and grief. It magnified my emotions, pain, and scars. It hurt me to my very core. I felt so deeply for her. What it must have been like, struggling to get free, knowing her time was up.

The following Sunday was July 2, viewing day. I made the long two hour drive to the funeral home and I arrived to an empty park lot as I was the first to arrive. I was greeted at the door by a gentle, older gentleman, and was told I could go in if I would like to. I slowly walked into the big room and peered up front to see where my wife lay. It is an unsettling sight to see someone you love like that for the first time. As I made the slow walk to the front of the room, I had the sensation that I were standing on a boat out to sea, with the waves gently rocking the boat from side to side. Struggling to keep my balance, I finally reached the casket and just starred at her lying there. I didn't touch her. I didn't talk to her. In my mind, I knew only her shell was present. It made it easier to know without a shadow of a doubt, that she was dancing with Jesus.

It wasn't long and family and friends started showing up. I stayed at the front near Kari, and greeted people, as they came by to give their last respects. I was overwhelmed by the support I received that day. Many friends, family, and coworkers, some traveling great distances, were there to bid their last farewell. As hard as it was for me to stay standing with an achy heart and rubber legs, I felt in some ways I had an advantage. I saw with my own eyes the reality of Kari's death. I still held the images in my mind of her lying there motionless under the tractor. I also lived with her every day. The first night she wasn't there, it quickly became very real to me. I knew Kari was gone. I had been grieving for days. Others were just now making the connection and were just starting the grieving process.

I had my parents bring Lauren to the funeral home with them but Luke stayed with a friend. Lauren seemed to do alright but she kept her distance from her mom. She walked up front and stood next to Kari for a brief moment but then it seemed that was all she could handle and she went away and stayed with family. She didn't cry but you could tell she was sad and disconnected. I suppose that is the only way she could deal with it.

After a six hour, tiresome day filled with many hugs and condolences, I left the funeral home alone. On the way home, I stopped off at the gas station where Kari worked when we first got married. I had often gone in to see her on her breaks when she worked night shifts, just to spend time with her. It was around 7pm and I was starving after the long emotional day, so I picked up some petroleum pizza out of the warmer near the register, and paid the young girl working, where Kari once stood.

On the lonely drive home, I had an empty feeling inside of me. I cried no real tears all day long but like the last time I made a trip to the funeral home, the two hour drive back to Greencastle was a brutal one. I cried most of the way home. One more day to get through was all that kept me going. It's not that I was at all trying to be disrespectful of Kari, but I hated the way I was feeling. I hated the whole process of funerals. I wanted to be left alone to grieve and all that led up to this moment was preventing me from fully doing that. I wanted to do it my way. When I got home I said my prayers, climbed into bed, and I cried myself to sleep.

The next day I awoke, showered, and got ready. It was funeral day. I made the hour trip to Lafayette wearing my uncomfortable suit and tie that I had just bought a few days before. I had decided to have the funeral there because Kari and I both had worked there and we had been going to church there for a couple of years. The funeral was to be at the church that we had attended and where Kari also drove the church bus for special functions and trips. We had made a lot of friends in Lafayette and I felt that would give some people that lived there, the opportunity to pay their respects if they couldn't make the trip to Elwood.

When I arrived at the church, I walked through the front door and was met with friends and family that had already arrived. I was having a lot of stomach issues that morning, as I think the stress was becoming too overwhelming for my body to handle. I hadn't taken any medications as I was just trying to rely on God to get me through. I needed an extra dose of his medicine to get me through the funeral.

Before the funeral service started, I was met by a pretty, young woman with a baby in a stroller. She handed me a greeting card and introduced herself to me. She said her name was Stephanie Dinn and she had heard about the accident through her friend that attended our church in Lafayette. Stephanie had attended the church just before Kari and I had started going there so we had never met. When Stephanie heard about the accident, she felt God led her to tell me about her church in Greencastle. I was touched to know a stranger drove an hour to tell me about her church and to share in my grief. I knew without a doubt, that I wanted to attend her church In Greencastle the following Sunday.

The funeral was an uplifting worship service filled with praise to God. I enjoyed the music and sang out to God with everything that I had. I felt a lot of mixed emotions during the service but I didn't cry. After the service my mom asked if I wanted to walk up and see Kari one last time. I refused to go up again. I told her that Kari was in heaven and that she wasn't there. As the old hymn says so beautifully, it was well, with my soul.

During the drive back to Elwood for the burial, I started to feel worse. I was overcome with my stomach sickness and had to stop at a gas station. After expelling things, I felt better and was able to continue on with the hour drive back to our old hometown.

When I arrived at the cemetery, I was surprised to see all that had made the drive back to Elwood for the quick graveside service. It is the small things like that, that make a huge difference for someone that has been through so much so quickly. I was grateful for all the love and support I was shown. I was glad Kari had made an impact on other people's lives.

After the service concluded, we all headed back to our old church in Elwood for the funeral dinner. I didn't have much of an appetite because of my upset stomach and only nibbled on a little food that was graciously prepared for us by the church. I talked with friends and family for a while about what my future held, and then it was time to get the kids and head home. A scary new chapter in my life was to begin; A chapter in my life that I was not ready for. There would be nothing to occupy my mind. There would be nothing to plan for. It was truly time to start the grieving process.

Psalm 23:4

Even though I walk through the valley of the shadow of death, I fear no evil; for Thou art with me; Thy rod and Thy staff, they comfort me. (NIV)

CHAPTER 5

25 DAYS OF HELL

The early grief process felt as if I was treading through the hot fires of hell with grotesque demonic beasts waiting to devour me if I stumbled and fell. Some days were better than others but I never got to leave hell. The demons were always trying to beat me down, take away my spirit and hope, and then ultimately destroy me. I had to fight with everything I had daily, to survive the attacks. At times, I felt as if I would succumb to their evil desires, at times I almost did. Thankfully I choose to surrender to God for His protection.

The funeral was now over, and now it was time to face reality; the reality that I was now a single dad in a town where I knew no one. My old life was over. I had to face a scary new life and I had to face it alone. I didn't know who was going to watch the kids while I worked. To compound the problem, I was working nightshift which would make things even more difficult to work out. I didn't have the answers or solutions; I only had my faith in God to carry me through. I clung to him dearly.

The first evening home proved to be the start of what was to come. I was in the bedroom when a wave of emotions came over me. As I began to cry, Lauren walked in and I quickly wiped the tears away. I thought I had to be strong for her. I now realize I was wrong. I needed to be strong yes, but I also needed to show her that feeling, crying, and grieving is normal and natural. She pretended to not notice and carried on like everything was ok. I was not.

I immediately started doing things to make a fresh start. I knew it wasn't going to be easy but I also knew there were things I could do to help me heal. I removed my wedding ring and put it in my top dresser drawer. I didn't feel any shame in doing so. I just didn't want to pretend. I was no longer married. I also started doing the little things that always annoyed Kari. I considered doing these things my way of moving on. I could be myself and there was no one I was going to bother. That new sense of freedom eased my burden just a bit.

That first week home it seemed that every day was the same. I would wake up in the morning with waves of pain and sadness. I would lie awake in bed and stare at the ceiling fan going round and round. I had no motivation, no energy, and no hope for a future. I felt incomplete like a part of me was missing. I had lost my best friend, the one person I would tell anything and everything to. I often found myself hearing about something and would think to myself, I can't wait to tell Kari that. Then it would hit me. That would never happen. My wife was dead.

Kari's dad came to visit the first day or two after I got home. As you can imagine, he was devastated. He tried to keep his mind and body busy by mowing the grass and doing other chores around the house. When he saw the tree stump in the front yard, he just stared at it. When I saw him standing there looking at it, I knew what we must do. Together, we went to the barn and found a hatchet. We dug at the base of the tree and started chopping. We must have been at it for half an hour when the neighbor across the road saw our struggles. He drove over in his backhoe, and in a few short swoops of the bucket, the stump was gone. It created a funny feeling in my stomach when the stump that created so much devastation was removed so easily. It gave us some type of feeling of accomplishment, but there was really nothing to fill up the empty feeling we had inside. No matter how hard we worked, we couldn't undue what had been done. We only wished that backhoe could fill our emptiness as easily as it did those holes in the ground.

Early on, my mom came and stayed with me for a few days. I was not a big fan of having someone there as I knew I needed to be alone to face my situation, but looking back, having someone there allowed me to do parts of the healing process that would have been much harder had she not been there. My mom cooked and cleaned for me and allowed me to just be. I spent many hours those first few days in the woods clearing trails. I chased the pain away by using a chainsaw in the hot summer heat. Clearing trails was something Kari and I had talked about doing so it was healing to get them done. It was healing to be alone.

I would often go out to Kari's white minivan, turn on the radio and just sit there. I didn't move or change anything. I listened to the station that she had playing when she turned the van off. It brought me comfort and peace to sit where she sat. The shower that she had bought on her last night did not move from its resting place in the back. I didn't have the will or energy to touch it.

Before my mom left, we talked about my future. She asked me what I was going to do and where I was going to live. She thought maybe I should move back to Elwood, the place where she and dad lived and the place I was born and raised. Right away I knew this was not the answer. Kari and I moved to Greencastle following our dream. To leave now would mean Kari had died for nothing. I knew it was going to be tough to stay. To walk across the ground where your best friend died has a way of ripping apart old wounds, but as hard as it was going to be, I knew what I had to do. I had to face it head on. I was going to stay.

My mom also thought it might be a good idea to see about getting some medications to help me out during the rough times. It was something that had never really crossed my mind. I knew I had my God and I knew he was enough to carry me through. It was important for me to feel every last bit of the hurt and pain. I knew, the sooner I felt it all, the sooner I could get through the valley and move on with my life. I wanted to laugh, smile, and be happy again and I knew time alone would not heal me. I had to do the work. There was no easy way out.

Not long after my mom left, my mother in law, Becky called. She said she would be able to stay for a few weeks to help out with the kids, if I wanted her to. My first reaction was to say no, but I was so occupied with my grief, I felt I couldn't be there for the kids like I needed to be. I knew I needed more time for myself to heal. I realized the help it had been when my mom was there and knowing I was not available to meet all my children's needs, I agreed to have her come stay for a bit. A couple days later, Becky made the long trip to Greencastle from Florida, and got settled in. It was Saturday and the following day would be the first Sunday since the funeral and I was eager to go to Stephanie's church. Even though I would know no one there, I was eager to feel the comfort of a church family.

Sunday July 9, 2006

For the first time since Kari died, I awoke to my alarm clock on Sunday morning with a bit of optimism. I couldn't wait to attend our new church and I was excited to praise God. After we all got ready to go, we made the 20 minute drive to the church and for the first time, I was attending a church as a single parent. I remember walking through the front door and sensing that everyone was looking at me. Not in a bad way, but I couldn't help but wonder if they knew about the accident. My suspicions were correct as I was quickly met by a young woman named Angela. She was in charge of meals for people in need in the congregation. She offered the service from the church and I agreed for them to bring meals out to the house. I felt a great sense of belonging to something even though I had not even attended a service. It was a much needed feeling.

After talking with Angela, I dropped Luke off at the nursery and Lauren off at her classroom and found my way to the church sanctuary. I found a seat in the back and got settled in. The church was a much larger church than I was used to. It was a newer building with high ceilings and bright lights. It had a gradually sloping floor toward the front with a large carpeted stage for worship music and preaching. I instantly felt at home and felt the love of so many of God's people. I loved the music we sang that day and we even sang a song I had picked out for Kari's funeral. I knew right away this is where I belonged. I was so thankful that God put Stephanie in my life and so glad she listened to him and made the trip to Lafayette.

Now that Becky was around, I immediately started taking more time for myself. She would often take the kids places so I would be alone for extended periods of time. I spent a lot of my free time reading the bible and grief books. I also started going on long three mile runs in the evenings, down my country road. I enjoyed the peace, scenery, and wildlife, as I made my way out to county line road and back. It felt good to get out and burn off stress and get a good sweat going but no matter how far I would run, I couldn't out run the pain. Evenings were always the worst for me. As darkness approached, feelings of sadness and loneliness would hit me hard. I often would make it the majority of the day with only nausea and stomach pains, but I always knew, like storm clouds rolling in, the tears would be on their way. Even though I knew it was coming, there was nothing I could do.

It was a bright and sunny day when I finally found the energy to empty out Kari's van. It was something that I had been putting off but I knew it had to be done. I opened the back of the van and unloaded the shower she bought, into the barn.   I thought sooner or later I would work on that bathroom and put that shower up but it never happened. That shower sat in the barn for years until the abuse from it being stacked up with other things on top of it, made it just like our shattered dreams, and it was eventually thrown in the trash.

Becky and I were invited to the city park with some people from my new church. This was the first time I would try socializing since the accident and I had my reservations about it. The whole time I was there I felt I didn't belong. Everyone was busy having a good old time with friends and I was alone and numb. One of the couples we met there was hanging all over each other and the young girl, with a big smile on her face stated, "We do everything together." It was a grim reminder of what I no longer had. I wanted out of there but I knew it wasn't all about me and reminded myself that the kids were having fun. As I looked over to find my kids among the other children playing, I spotted Luke and Lauren on top of a giant wooden, toy tractor, with Luke pretending like he was driving. My stomach instantly dropped as I started having flashbacks.

I am forever scarred by what I saw on the afternoon of June 27th, 2006. I replayed what must have happened, hundreds and hundreds of times in my mind. I couldn't shake it. I couldn't get it out of my mind. I was often in the middle of conversations, or would be thinking about something else, and it would jump into my mind and I couldn't get it out. I would see Kari lying there with the tractor on top of her. It would turn my stomach. The memory followed me everywhere I went. Seeing Luke and Lauren on that tractor crushed what was left of my broken spirit.

At the end of our time at the park, Angela from my new church was asking what Luke would want for his birthday. She had taken it upon herself to organize his second birthday party and for that, I was very grateful. She asked, "Does he like toy tractors?" At this, I knew it was time to go. I just couldn't take it anymore. I was mentally and emotionally drained. We quickly left and Becky and I both agreed it was too soon to partake in such things.

I struggled with so many things early on but I think the thing that bothered me most was my longing for intimacy, an intimacy I couldn't have. I started to feel a clinginess about me when I was around women. It unsettled me greatly. I knew I was weak. I started having dreams, bad dreams. One night I dreamt I kissed a woman. I didn't know who this woman was, but I know I kissed her. I awoke with so much guilt and shame, I cried. I felt it was so disrespectful to Kari that I even dreamed such a thing. I prayed that God take it from me.

I had many visitors come to the house the first few weeks, many traveled great distances to get there. The pastor and his wife from the church Kari and I had just starting attending the past two Sundays before her death, made the 30 minute drive to the house. We had great discussion and for the first time, I started to think about my future. I told the pastor, "I don't know why this happened and I don't understand why God would allow it to but maybe there is a single mother out there somewhere that really needs my help. I am certainly not thinking about that now, I am only thinking about the possibilities of God's plan." This was an important step for me and it gave me hope, a hope I desperately needed. Kari and I had talked a few times about the what if's. When you talk about those things, you never think they are going to happen but I am so glad we did. We had both agreed the other should move on with their lives and remarry if the opportunity presented itself. She also often had said she wished she would die before me because she didn't think she could take going on without me. It is not the kind of thing you like to talk about, but having had those conversations gave me great peace moving forward with my future, a future without my wife.

As the days went by, I noticed that the numbness was wearing off. Numbness had gotten me through the funeral and protected me early, but as time went on, the pain got worse. Memories started becoming clearer. I started recalling conversations with Kari like they just happened. I thought of our last kiss on the porch as I was leaving for work, and recalled our last words we spoke to each other when I arrived home from work. I remembered so clearly Kari's words on the swing that day by the creek, "I think I am going to like it here." I was having feelings of guilt and I often wondered why I was alive and Kari was dead. I constantly had tears in my eyes. I was hurting so bad.

I decided now, as the pain was getting worse by the day, was a good time to start counseling so Lauren and I started going. I had seen a counselor in the past and I wanted to stay with someone I was familiar with so I made the 90 minute drive to Anderson once a week. My time there was healing. Kari and I both had been to see her and she knew us quite well. I felt good to talk with someone that knew Kari and it was healing to express myself to her. After I had been to her 3 or 4 times, she spoke up to me and said, "You know Jason; you have really good coping skills." I wasn't sure what to make of the comment as I felt I was often one step away from losing it, but it did make me feel good to hear it. It did give me hope.

The pain of everyday living was often more than I could bear. It made me stir crazy. I often made trips into town. I had no reason to go but I just couldn't sit still. The kids and I would often travel to Wal-Mart just to be around people or to spend money to try to make myself feel better. I would spend hours in that place, walking aimlessly, filled with sadness and depression. People would be smiling and laughing, going 100 miles an hour and it felt like I was standing still. I felt like the old man going down the highway doing 45 miles per hour, that everyone wants to pass. I had no place to go, no place to be, and no one waiting on me to get home.

I was headed into Wal-Mart, like I often did, one afternoon. This was actually my second trip into town that day. I hadn't heard from anyone in awhile and I had been crying a lot throughout the day. I hurt. This was a particularly bad day in hell. I was about half way into town when we came upon a really sharp curve in the road, the kind of curve that you have to slow down to 20 miles per hour for. Just as we started to enter the curve a speeding pickup truck swerved in front of the car, narrowly missing hitting us head on. I felt as if I were dreaming. I looked in the rear view mirror but there was nothing. I started to panic. Again, I looked in the rear view mirror and nothing. I asked Lauren, "Did you see the truck? Where did it go"? She shrugged her shoulders with a puzzled look on her face so I pulled the car off the side of the road and got out. I was physically shaking and trembling as I approached where I had last seen the truck. There was a steep drop off along the side of the road, and in the bottom rested the truck, upside down. I didn't see anyone moving. The truck was just still. I didn't know what to do. I couldn't do anything. I started to go into shock. I started having flashbacks of Kari's accident. My heart raced. My mind was not there. I just stood there in the road motionless, peering down at the truck, doing nothing. At that moment, a truck coming down the road saw something was wrong and pulled off the road and got out. I frantically tried to tell him what had happened but I struggled to get my words out clearly. He finally got the message and dialed 911. Moments later, an ambulance arrived to access the situation. As it turns out, he somehow was able to walk away from the crash, extremely shaken, but ok. Lauren, Luke and I went ahead and went into town after that but I was shaken the rest of the day. My head was spinning and my stomach was twisted all sorts of ways. I was so tired. I was so weak. I wanted a break from it all but when you are grieving, there is no break. You just keep fighting; you keep going because that is all you can do.

The following day I started going through things and found some good pictures of Kari and I cried uncontrollably. It was as if seeing the pictures made it all that more real for me. I found our family picture and hung it on the living room wall. I went through boxes that were yet to be unpacked and found Kari's coats. I cried and cried as I searched the pockets and found receipts to her favorite stores, Big Red bubble gum, and change. I cried at the thought that she had put that stuff there. I held the coats to my face, smelled them all, and then cried some more. As I got ready for bed that night, I looked over and saw Kari's pillows still lying there. I picked them up and just held them tight. I smelled them one last time and then took them off the bed. It was so very hard to do but it was another necessary step for me. I knew it had to be done. I wrote this prayer in my journal as I lie in bed:

"God give me strength to do this. I miss Kari so much. I am so alone. I so long for her embrace it scares me sometimes. I feel so vulnerable right now. I feel so clingy. I have to keep my distance from women. My head is just so messed up. I just have to turn to you. You are all that

I have. I can't wait to get through this valley so I can help others. That's all that matters to me now. I want to be a blessing to others. Life is so short. I need to live every minute of every day. Every day is a gift from you."

I awoke the next day with a positive attitude. It was a new day and I thought it was going to start getting easier. I was wrong. This day would prove to be my hardest day yet. I received a phone call from the funeral home to tell me they had gotten the death certificate and that they would mail it out to me. That phone call hit me right between the eyes. I am not sure why, but it seemed to make it even more real. I was receiving a certificate to tell me my wife was dead. I hung up the phone and began to cry. No matter how hard I tried, I couldn't control my emotions. I hurt 100 times more than I ever had in my life.

After I settled down a bit, I made my trip to Wal-Mart. I Walked around aimlessly, and then cried all the way home. On the way home, I looked over at the fire station, where the tractor was being stored, and it had been moved. It was now in plain sight behind the building. The sight of the tractor caused a rush of pain and sadness that overwhelmed me beyond words, and I started screaming in the car. I was beat down, broken, tired and drained and I couldn't handle it anymore. I had nothing left in me.

As evening approached, I saw a storm was about to break out. I knew I may get wet, but I wanted to do my evening run anyway as it had become part of my routine. I set out on my run and it wasn't very long before the lightning started flashing and the dark, dreary weather seemed to drag me down even further. I was overrun with depression and sadness. I felt I didn't want to live anymore. I asked God to take me. I pleaded with him, "Please God take me from this place." I desperately wanted to see Kari again and I felt the pain was too much to bear. I cried and I cried as the rain poured down on me.

When I returned from my run, the tears continued in the shower. It was a scary time for me as it was the most out of control I had felt. I couldn't contain my tears. I had no control over my emotions. I stepped out of the shower and looked at the man starring back at me. I didn't look good. I didn't look good at all. I noticed for the first time I had grey hairs coming in. This sank me further into depression. I got dressed and regained some composure before walking through the living room where Becky and the kids were. I said goodnight and climbed the stairs to bed. It took me a long time to get to sleep. I lie in bed and continued to cry until I ran out of tears.

The next morning the kids, grandma, and I had plans to go fishing. We had been invited by the fire department chaplain that I had met shortly after Kari died. The pond was just up the road from our house and it had been a while since I had been around a lot of people, so I decided to try the social thing once again. When we pulled up around noon, there were several people already there from the chaplain's church. They were having a cookout and I could smell the delicious aroma as soon as I stepped out of the car. The sun was shining, the fish were biting, and the kids were having fun. We were having a great time. For a little while, I almost forgot about the pain and sadness in my life. That quickly changed when it came time to leave. Becky decided to take the kids into town so I went home alone. Having a bit of fun that day was like a dam holding back a gigantic lake. As I got home to an empty house, that dam broke and I was flooded with pain and sadness like I hadn't felt before. It was more than I could take. I thought it would be a good idea to take all my frustrations and pain out on a good workout. I had lifted weights for years but hadn't been working out since the accident. The workout quickly turned into a screaming fest. I had fits of rage, bouts of sadness, and unbearable pain. I was all over the place with my emotions. I threw the weights. I started trembling.

After working out, I went upstairs and grabbed some pictures of Kari. I sat in our red leather chair and looked at them, and then began to ball hysterically. I screamed and cried and cried and screamed. I got out of the chair and screamed some more. I screamed so loud I was nervous the neighbors 100 yards away may hear. I paced the floor and then fell back into the chair. I shook uncontrollably. I punched things. I broke things. There was now where I could go. I couldn't get comfortable. I couldn't control the pain. I didn't know what to do. In desperation I called my friends Desiree and Joel. My hands shook as I dialed their number. I don't remember much of the conversation as I was pretty out of it but Desiree was able to comfort me. She asked if I needed them to come over. Had they been across town I am sure I would have jumped at the offer but with the distance that separated us, I didn't want to burden them. I hung up the phone and went for a ride on the four wheeler through the woods. I talked to God a lot on that ride and he gave me a break from the pain. When I got back to the house, I went inside and I dropped to my knees. I begged God to take my hurt and pain away. I cried out to him with everything I had and he gave me peace.

That evening I went for my run like I always did and I cried not one tear. I made it all the way home without being overcome with sadness. As the daylight turned to dark, I was ok. I showered and climbed the stairs to bed. It had been over four hours since I had shed a tear. I was at peace.

As I lie in bed I prayed to God. My attention turned to the kids. I wanted to get better for them. I wanted to be an awesome dad for them. I wanted them to know that I drew my strength not from myself but from Jesus Christ. I prayed that I never forget that God is always first, number one. He is all that really matters. The things of this earth don't matter. We are only here for a little while and then we move on. If we believe in him, we don't die, we move on to the good stuff.

Mathew 11:28

Come to me, all you who are weary and
burdened, and I will give you rest. **(NIV)**

CHAPTER 6

A ROLLER COASTER

The following day was filled with comfort
and peace. There were very few tears. I got a
break from flashbacks from the accident. I
started thinking happy thoughts. I started to get
excited for my job interview that I had the next
day. I started thinking about happy memories. I
started thinking less about what Kari missed out
on, and more about what she was experiencing
now. I imagined what it must be like in heaven
and I pictured Kari there having the time of her
life. When I started to feel my heartache coming
on, I instantly dropped to my knees again and
begged God for his help. I felt his presence and I
was given peace.

I awoke the next morning with more
positivity. I was energized about my interview. I
had directions written down that I received from
one of the interviewers over the telephone. I

showered, got dressed, and then grabbed my car keys and directions from the kitchen counter. My emotions were starting to get the best of me and I started to get a bit nervous as I neared downtown Indianapolis. I knew the importance of the interview and what it would mean if I got the job.

I had no problems finding the correct building and when I arrived, I was met in the front lobby by a fellow employee dressed in an all white uniform. He checked me through security and walked me down a long, dark, narrow hallway toward their work area. When we arrived there, I was taken inside a very small, dimly lit room not much bigger than a closet. I was there for only a minute before the first of four interviewers came in. The only interviewer to mention anything about Kari's death was the first young woman that walked in. It was all I could do to hold back tears and emotions when she offered her condolences. I was hoping with everything that I had, it wouldn't be brought up. I needed to concentrate on my task at hand. I just wanted to be treated normal for the day.

After a grueling interview process, I got to tour the buildings to see exactly what went on in the facility. I visualized myself working there and I liked what I saw. I left the interviews with a positive feeling about the day. I felt I had represented myself well and I just had to wait and see if I fit what they were looking for. I hoped and prayed I would get the job.

The next few days after the interview were filled with hope and optimism. I could feel the tide turning. I started feeling more positive and more upbeat. I started to see a small glimmer of hope in the dark, dark place that was my life. I became thankful for the time I had with Kari. In the 12 years I knew her, she changed me in so many ways. I am who I am now because of things she taught me and she continues to teach me through her death.

Kari was a loving and giving person. She always went out of her way to help people in need. There are countless examples but one that stands out in mind was her heart for the elderly. Whenever we would go grocery shopping and she would see an elderly person loading groceries, she would run over to them and help load them and put their cart up for them. To be honest, it made me embarrassed when she did that, but her caring heart and generosity has made an impact on my life.

As good as having a bit of hope felt, I knew the walk through the valley was far from over. Just a few short days later, I started struggling again. I remained focused on my future but my fatigue and weakness were really starting to affect me. I was tired, so very tired. I had no motivation. I started noticing my confidence was really shaken. When I had a bad day, there was no one there to lift me up. When I needed to talk to someone about something important, there was no one to turn to. The short break from the pain was officially over as the accident scene began creeping back into my mind again. I would replay it over and over. I would walk into the front yard and I would see the tractor upside down. I would see Kari trying to get free. The fresh reminder was still visible as you could still see the fresh dirt exposed where the tractor tires spun in the grass. Every time I went out there, my heart would sink and I would feel sick to my stomach. I often went to that spot in the yard to pray.

I awoke the next day with Luke crying and talking in his bed. I didn't want to get up. I waited for the last possible minute when he became really fussy before I got him. I stood up out of bed and I could feel the weakness in my legs. Had it not been for the kids, I don't think I would have gotten up that day. I was so depressed, tired, and drained. "Another wonderful day," I sarcastically said to myself as I started the day.

Later that day Becky took the kids into town. I was home alone, when I received a knock on the front door. I had contacted an excavator to do some work at the house a few shorts weeks before Kari died. Two men, a father and son, had come out to the house and Kari and I told them what we wanted done. They were scheduled to do the work the day after the accident, but after hearing about it, they left us alone.

When they arrived, they asked if I still needed the work done and I told them I sure did. I went outside and watched as they proceeded to work with their heavy machinery for four hours in the hot, humid, summer heat. The project turned out great and I was very thankful for the job they had done. As they were finishing, I went inside to get my checkbook. I was expecting the bill to be somewhere around 400-500 dollars. I met them back outside as they had just finished up their work and were walking to their truck. "How much do I owe you," I asked. With a gentle and sincere look in his eyes, the younger man said, "You don't owe us anything. It is our gift to you." I immediately felt God's presence and was overrun with a sense of his love. The first time they were out to access the job we had talked about faith and I knew they were both Christians. I knew God was sending his people to show us love and comfort us. I felt his arms around me tight.

After I went inside, I went into the kitchen to cook some lunch when I heard a knock on the door. It was a volunteer fireman from the fire station up the road. A young man he knew had displayed interest in the tractor and he wanted to know if I wanted to sell it. He told me that it would need some work because the steering wheel was bent so he adjusted the price for the damages. I had no idea how much it was worth so I trusted him to be fair. I agreed upon his price and he said he would be back. Even though the money would be helpful, I just wanted to get that thing out of my life. I thought it would be nice to not have to see that thing sitting at the station again. I was ready to move forward. Later that same day, he came back with the cash in hand and I thanked him for taking his time to help me out with it. I felt relieved that it was gone.

The following day I was driving into town. I was just about to the fire station when I saw it. At the house right next to the fire station, was the old tractor. Now, instead of being parked behind a building, it was parked in his front yard right by the road. Seeing it there was so hard to swallow. Tears instantly welled up in my eyes. My mind quickly flashed back to the accident where it stayed the remainder of the day. As much as I wanted it out of my life, I had no choice but to face it head on. I couldn't avoid it.

With the local county fair in full swing, Becky and I had decided to take the kids. It was a hot sunny, late July afternoon as I pushed Luke through the grass in his stroller. The smell of elephant ears was filling the air with their golden fried goodness. Becky and I watched as Lauren was all smiles going from one ride to the next. As I watched Lauren having fun, my emotions began to get to me and I had to wipe my eyes often to keep them dry.

Lauren came up to me and pleaded with me, with her beautiful green eyes, to ride something with her. After some poking and prodding, I agreed to one ride. My stomach wasn't feeling all that well to begin with so flying through the air, going round and round, only worsened my condition. After I wobbly stepped off the ride, I took a seat on a wooden bench near a trash can, and did not move for a good fifteen minutes until my stomach settled down enough to get up.

From the rides we proceeded into the 4h building to look at all the projects in there. As we were walking past the displays, my eyes were drawn to a project done by a young boy about tractor safety. I stopped dead in my tracks, and started reading. It had a diagram of a tractor with a safety bar and told about its importance to the driver of the tractor. I felt like I had been hit by a train when I saw it. When we bought that tractor, I knew nothing about them. I didn't know of any dangers and I certainly didn't know of the existence of safety bars. I walked away from that display feeling ignorant, and I was filled with an intense anger of that ignorance.

The following day I was reminded that Becky and the kids were leaving to go to church camp. I was going to have a lot of quiet time at home. I instantly became nervous as I wasn't sure how I would handle the alone time. I knew it was something I needed but it still made me uneasy. I was scared to be by myself. With Becky and Lauren gathering their things and still at the house, I was in my bedroom going through Kari's belongings. I found a note in Kari's dresser from Lauren. It read, "I love you Mom and I like you more than flowers, Love Lauren." It was the first time I had seen the note and it broke my heart and I started crying. It was just the other day when Luke said his first sentence. I had just put a shirt on him and he said, "That looks nice." My heart broke at the thought that Kari wasn't here to see the kids grow up. My heart broke at the thought that the kids wouldn't have their mom with them. I would often watch them sleep at night before I would go to bed and I would cry. They were so innocent yet this bad and sinful world took their mommy from them. It just didn't seem fair.

My first day at home by myself was a good one. I felt a bit of positivity and confidence coming back in me. It was refreshing and I welcomed it with open arms. I knew I didn't have a choice in it and I certainly didn't ask for Kari to die, but I knew for the first time since the accident, I would not fail. My life could have purpose again. I was still alive so I knew God still had a plan for me. I wasn't sure what that purpose was, but I knew I would honor him with whatever it was. By the end of the day, not one tear drop had fallen. I could have cried a few times but it didn't happen. I was so thankful for the break from the intense pain. It's not that I missed Kari any less, but I had leaned on God and he held me up. I felt God's hands upon me.

As I was sitting at home alone that day, I started thinking about Lauren and Luke and how much I loved them. I wasn't worried about them having the best this or that, or what college they would attend. I didn't care if they played sports or what activities they liked. I worried about them knowing and loving God. Nothing else mattered to me. This was a new revelation for me. In just a few short months, my whole perspective on life had changed. I had changed.

The next few days were filled with many tears and sadness. I seemed to be on a rollercoaster ride of emotions. Some days were better than others but they all hurt. New memories were coming to me all the time. I would drive by a restaurant or a store and a memory that happened there would smack me in the face. The emotions I was feeling were indescribably painful. I started asking myself questions. Will I ever marry again? Could I ever marry again? Would I ever have a heart I could give away again? My heart was so shattered and broken. I wasn't sure if it could ever heal.

Kari's friend Desiree and her husband Joel invited me over for supper the following Friday evening. I looked forward to the opportunity to see them so the kids and I made the hour long trip to Lafayette. We had a lot of fun that night and I seemed to forget, for a brief moment, the pain I was in. We talked and talked, and talked some more and we finally ended up leaving at midnight. Outside of God, they were my rock in the early days of my grief. Before Kari died, I hardly even knew them. Now they were propping me up in my darkest hour. I truly believe they were sent from God to help me during my journey.

As the days wore on, I still had trouble wrapping my mind around the truth. My mind did not want to believe that Kari was gone. I was still in shock. I had waves of pain and sadness that would hit me out of nowhere. I still had intense bouts of crying and fits of rage. I would scream and yell, and cry out to God to help me. I still had days I cried all day long. I wondered when things would get better. I felt I couldn't take anymore. Some days I felt I was too tired to go on. It was all I could do to make it through each day.

I received a phone call from a friend I met at church while Kari and I lived in Lafayette. He asked me if I wanted to meet him for lunch and I welcomed the opportunity to meet with him. I made the trip to Lafayette and met him at Kari and I's favorite restaurant. I felt an eerie feeling as I pulled into the busy parking lot. I hadn't been there since right before Kari and I left town for our move to Greencastle. I felt uncomfortable and got that sick feeling in my stomach as I walked through the double doors. It was a happy environment with upbeat music playing and smiling door greeters, but I instantly had an extreme feeling of loneliness. It was a familiar place that Kari and I had visited often and this time she was not there. I felt empty.

It wasn't long and my friend showed up. He had made a lot of phone calls to me during the last month and I was thankful for his friendship and that he had asked me to lunch. After a short wait, our names were called and the waitress had us follow her to our seats. It just so happens that we were seated right next to the seat Kari and I sat at the last time we were there. I immediately felt uncomfortable.

I remembered our last meal there so well. I still remembered the conversations we had in that both about our dream in Greencastle. We couldn't wait to get there and start our new life. Little did we know, our dream was almost over. As our meal arrived, I became even more distracted and I couldn't help but stare at the both where we had sat. I must have been a boring friend that day as my mind was not present. I struggled through my time there and somehow made it through the meal but was so glad when it was time to leave. The day did not at all go like I had planned. I was hoping that with visiting with my friend, some of the emptiness I was felling would be filled up but I left that restaurant feeling even more drained than when I got there. I drove home from Lafayette with a hollow feeling and void in my heart. That night I made a journal entry like I always did when the day was over. It was very healing to write out my prayers and thoughts at the end of the day. Here is what I wrote 45 days after Kari's death:

"I can't believe Kari is dead. I am so depressed, so broken hearted. I am exhausted. I have nothing left. I'm running out of tears. How long can this go on and how painful can this get? How much can a person take? When does it get easier? I loved Kari more than words can describe. She and I had become one. Now I am off balance because I am missing part of me. I feel I can hardly stand up now. Every task I do is difficult. I feel borderline insane. I need a break so bad but there are no

breaks. Each day flows into the next like one long nightmare. I've often noticed in graveyards when one spouse dies the other spouse dies soon thereafter. I understand how it could kill you. I am ready to go home whenever God takes me. Until then Lord, use my hands for your work. Thank you for today."

I had put it off for as long as I could but the following day, Lauren was to start school, so I needed to take her clothes shopping. I assumed that it was going to be a hard day but I really didn't know what I was in for. When it came to clothes shopping for the kids, I had always been completely hands off. I didn't have a clue. My time at the store was filled with an overwhelming sensation of loneliness and despair. It is at times like these, that the absence of your wife and the reality of your situation, truly hits you hard. It was an extremely painful time for me.

After we arrived, we made our way through the store and found the girls section. Without knowing what to do, I jumped right in and started combing the racks looking for clothes that I guessed were about Laurens size. As I tried to pick out outfits the best I could, I became dizzy and felt like my head was spinning. I became overwhelmed with the thought that this is how it's always going to be. Every time I turned around in the small isles, I was bumping into people. They had the clothes racks packed in so tight; there wasn't much space to move. There were so many people around and they were all moving so fast. I felt as if I were in slow motion. Everywhere I looked I saw moms shopping with their children. Some had their husbands with them, only their husbands were always hanging back ten feet behind them, not really paying attention to what was going on. That used to be me.

I had no idea what size to buy so I had Lauren turn around so I could check the tags in what she was wearing. As I was checking, I felt a tear run down my cheek. I wiped it away and regained my composure while Lauren was still turned around. She seemed to be ok with me doing the shopping and didn't seem to realize just how clueless I was. I was so very clueless. After spending what seemed like an eternity picking out clothes and going through the checkout line, I asked Lauren about her new clothes we had gotten. With excitement in her voice, she told me how much she loved them all. My six year olds validation of her new clothes helped to ease my tired and worried mind. I felt relief that it was over.

The following morning was August 15, Laurens' first day of first grade and it would be the first time she would stay at school all day. It was a day that Kari had long been looking forward to. I woke her up and started getting her ready. With little Luke still asleep in bed, I picked out Laurens clothes, fixed her breakfast, and tried the best I could to fix her hair. I grabbed my camera and took some pictures to remember the day.

After Lauren was ready, I woke Luke up so we could go down to the bus stop. It was a walk that I was not looking forward to. A new chapter was beginning in Laurens's life and Kari was not there to see it. It saddened me deeply to experience it by myself. Kari was supposed to be driving Lauren to school in her school bus like she had done the year before. Today, a stranger would be driving Lauren. After waiting for a few minutes, the bus pulled in front of our drive. I hugged and kissed Lauren and watched her get on the bus, and then Luke and I made the slow, depressing, 300 foot, walk back to the house.

I was in a great deal of depression all morning long. I realized then that there were going to be all sorts of things happen in the kids' lives that Kari was going to miss. I felt so much pain for my kids. I was beaten down. All my dreams had been shattered. I started wondering if I would ever recover from the scars. I wondered if I would ever be right again. I wondered if I would die from a broken heart.

Those next few days I again started seeing the accident more and more. I couldn't get it out of my head. It would replay over and over on a continuous loop. I would see the tractor flip and I would watch Kari die. I would see the tractor on top of her and I would try and try to get to move it, but I couldn't.

It was Friday afternoon August 18, when I received a phone call from my contact on the new job. He told me I had gotten the job I had interviewed for. I hung up the phone and cried like a baby. I had been on night shift for nine long years. Kari had wanted me on day shift for so very long. She was so excited at the thought I might be on days soon and today she would have been celebrating. I was relieved that I got the job because it answered a lot of my questions I had for taking care of the kids. I knew it was answered prayer but it also hurt so badly, so deep down. I was now going on day shift but Kari wasn't there to be with me. I felt relief and sadness at the same time. It was bittersweet.

That evening, the kids and I had planned on going to the local high school football game and out to eat. In our short time in Greencastle, Kari had quickly fallen in love with Marvin's, a restaurant in town. We had gotten it on several occasions and the kids and I enjoyed the pizza so that is where I wanted to take them. It was painful to walk through those doors for the first time without her, but I also knew there was healing with doing so. As the kids and I were getting seated in our booth by the window, I felt other people looking at us. It made me uneasy. It made me feel like a divorced dad that had just picked his kids up for the weekend. I felt like a failure. I had always prided myself on working hard on my marriage. I thought my marriage would never end. But here I was alone with the kids on a Friday night and I didn't like it.

Lauren and I were sitting there talking shortly after ordering our food, when Luke raised his arm, pointed to a girl next to us, and started saying one of the few words he knew, "Mom, Mom, Mom." My stomach dropped like I had just went down a giant hill on a roller coaster. I hadn't noticed it but a blonde haired young woman had sat down in the next both over and from the back, she did look like Kari. I started tearing up as I tried to pull Luke's hand down. As soon as I pulled his hand down, back up it went and again he said, "Mom, Mom, Mom." My heart ached for him. I didn't know what to do. I told him it was not Mom but he didn't understand and kept saying it. Finally, his attention was drawn to the food as it was brought to our table. I wiped away my tears and sat there for the next thirty minutes trying to put on a happy face for my kids.

After we finished off the pizza, we left Marvin's and headed to the game just a short drive down the road. We stopped at the concession stand after Lauren insisted, and got some popcorn before heading to our seats. The kids seemed to enjoy the game but I wasn't really there. I enjoyed the atmosphere of it all, as I love going to football games, but I was too busy thinking about what had just happened to enjoy myself. I sat there wondering what thoughts really go through Luke's mind. I wondered if he ever thought about where his mom went.

Saturday was a busy day filled with shopping and house cleaning so I didn't have much time to grieve. It was a welcomed day of mental rest for me. Not that you could ever fully rest, but to have a day to occupy your mind with something else, was nice. But as the ongoing nightmare continued, Saturday quickly turned into Sunday, and Sunday was not a good day.

While going through more things and trying to organize the house, I stumbled upon Kari's black, Nikon camera. I sat down in a soft chair and hesitantly turned it on. I started looking at the pictures and immediately began to sob. They were the last pictures she took. They were pictures I hadn't seen before. One of which, was a family picture from Easter Sunday at church. It was our last family picture. I was overtaken with incredible pain and sadness and stayed sitting in that chair for what seemed like hours. I cried, and cried, and cried some more and begged God to take the pain away. As I wobbly got up from the chair, I started to feel a new emotion. I was filled with an intense anger. I didn't know where it came from but I could feel it growing. I started getting mad at Kari. I hated that she left me alone with the kids. I hated that she didn't listen to me when I told her I would take care of that tree stump. I was mad at the pain. I was mad that I was so tired and worn out. I was mad at God. I knew at this moment, that I needed to face all of it head on. No more running, no more hiding, I must face the incredible pain head on.

The new week was a carbon copy of all the rest. More heartache, more tears, and more questions. I had spoken with my mom on the phone and I think she could tell I was so very worn out. She had agreed to make the two hour drive to pick the kids up on Friday. As much as I loved the kids, I was looking forward to more alone time. I was looking forward to spending more time concentrating on healing.

My mom and my older sister Tammy were to meet me and the kids at Lauren's school for her class picnic Friday evening. It turned out to be a beautiful sunny evening with pleasant temperatures, the perfect weather for the event. While Lauren was off playing on the playground, I ran into a nice young woman I recently met while trying to find Luke a babysitter. She was showing me a great deal of attention but I was so not ready for such things. I was flattered but never thought twice about it. I was still so very broken.

The weekend alone was filled with heartache and sadness. I longed for Kari so much. I was flooded with vivid memories. I cleaned out Kari's little black purse and I cried. I cried during church service. I cried when a church member brought two coolers full of meals out to the house. I watched my Jeremy Camp worship video, like I often did, and cried. I wondered if I would ever run out of tears. As I lie in bed on Sunday evening, I wrote this in my grief journal:

August 27, 2006

"Two months ago today, my wife, best friend, best buddy, my everything, left earth for heaven. Sometimes I think maybe I put too much of myself in one spot. Then when something happens to that one thing, you're left with nothing. I think Kari and I did too much together. Look at me now. I'm lost."

James 1:17

Every good gift and every perfect gift is from above, coming down from the Father of lights with whom there is no variation or shadow due to change. (NIV)

CHAPTER 7

A NEW BEGINNING

Upon waking the next day, I went into town to check my email at the library. I didn't have internet at home yet so going to the library had become part of my routine. It was always so nice to receive emails from friends and family. It kept me going. This particular morning was different. I noticed an email from someone that I wasn't familiar with. Her name was Fawn and she was writing to provide instructions for the meal she had made for me and the kids as part of my church's outreach. As I read the email, I quickly noticed her wit and humor and for the first time since Kari had died, I laughed. I laughed out loud right there in the quiet library. I had many people glance my way but I didn't care. For a brief moment, I felt something other than pain.

The rest of the day was filled with more tears but through all the pain, I continued to feel hope. The thought that Kari was with God in heaven enabled me to get up each morning and it enabled me to laugh and smile. I knew I would get better. I had so much to be thankful for. I started getting excited about life and it felt so good to feel something other than constant pain for a change. My new job was to start soon and I was looking forward to adding meaning and purpose to my life. It was to be a new beginning, a new chapter in my life. I felt through all the pain of the last two months, I had healed a great deal and because of God, I was ahead of where I could be. I was thankful for that.

The stress of finding Luke a babysitter was really starting to weigh on me as my start date for work was approaching fast. I was in my insurance agent's office talking about my situation when one of the employees there mentioned her daughter baby set. I didn't know her daughter, or the lady for that matter, but I didn't really have any choice. I had checked with some daycares around town and there were no openings available at the time. I wrote her number down and called her when I got home. Later that day I drove to her house to meet her. It was an uncomfortable meeting between us as we talked about Luke staying there. I felt as if I was interviewing her and in a way, I guess I was. She seemed pleasant and I agreed to have Luke stay there the following week but as I left, I had an uneasy feeling in me. I suppose that was only normal given the situation that I had to leave my baby with a stranger.

As September rolled around, I started going a whole day at a time without crying much and I wasn't sure what to make of that. Sometimes I just felt I was out of tears and out of emotions. Sometimes when I would start to smile I would feel guilty. Sometimes I felt guilty for not crying.

At church the next Sunday, I got to meet Fawn at church. She worked in the nursery so I handed Luke off to her when I arrived. I thought she seemed nice as she greeted me with a pleasant smile but I didn't think anymore about her. Even though I already felt a bit of chemistry and connection between us, I knew I was far from ready for a relationship. I knew I was a wounded man.

Tuesday, September 5, was my first day at work. I awoke with butterflies in my stomach as it had been three months since I had worked and today was the start of a new job. I had worked out plans to drop Lauren off at her friend's house at 6am and then drop Luke off at his babysitters by 6:30, and be at work by 7:30am. The drop-offs went seamless and I arrived at work on time.

The first few weeks at work went slow as I could only train when people were available to help me. The slow times gave me a lot of time to think. Whenever I would think, I would be overrun with painful memories and emotions. Even though I enjoyed my new job, it actually made things harder on me. I had too much downtime with nothing to do. I started seeing the accident again and I couldn't stop thinking about it. The tears started flowing a lot more. I started having more trouble with controlling my anger and I felt more anger towards my children. I started to get more depressed. I was so looking forward to starting my new job and in some ways, it was truly a blessing. At the same time, I felt I was regressing a bit with my healing and I didn't like that at all. I began to feel overwhelmed again as I didn't have as much time to spend with God like I had done before. I felt I had no purpose and I couldn't have a purpose as I had no energy to commit to one. I was just surviving from one day to the next. I felt I needed a vacation from it all.

As the days wore on and the routine of being back at work started wearing on me, I began to get rundown from trying to keep up with everything at home. My days were long with a ninety minute commute each way to work. The housework started to become more than I could handle. Friends were calling less and less. I was alone, sad, and depressed. This was my double dip into the grief valley. I was at bottom again.

One day, as I sat at my desk on lunch break, a wave of sadness overcame me. I began to think about Kari and how I missed her dearly. I wanted to hold her again but I knew that it would never happen. I couldn't contain my emotions and I didn't know what to do. I wanted to run and scream but I couldn't as I had coworkers all around. I wiped the tears away that started to form and quickly made my way to the restroom. When I got there, I locked myself in a bathroom stall and cried. I stayed there until I could regain my composure and then walked back to my desk hoping nobody noticed my red eyes.

I again turned to God for help and started focusing on him more. Between my commute and my time before bed, I was spending three to four hours a day in worship and prayer. I began to feel relief from the sadness and pain. I started to find a new normal. I was still lonely and in a lot of pain but things started getting better. The pain started lessoning and my hope started growing. I knew God was healing me. As the days turned into weeks, I started turning to exercise more and more. I started working out regularly again and began to lose weight. I found a Christian website online where I met some really nice people. Even though it was just through typing, it was wonderful to have people to share in my grief. It helped a great deal. With each passing day, I started to feel more whole. I started to be able to function again. I started thinking about my future. I now felt I could re marry someday. I had read in books to give yourself a year to grieve minimum before entering into a relationship, so I set that as my rule and would tell people that if they asked. I certainly was not looking for a girlfriend or a wife; I just knew someday I could give my heart away again. I would give it away in God's time.

The next six weeks things continued to improve. My tears began to dry up and crying became an exception rather than the rule. I got better and better at keeping up at home. My everyday exhaustion was replaced with more vigor and energy. My optimism and motivation for life continued to increase daily. I started setting goals and making plans. Life started to get exciting. I was finally at peace with everything. I didn't particularly like being a single parent but I was OK with it. My feelings of shame went away when I would take the kids out somewhere. I no longer felt like a divorced dad and I didn't care how anyone else perceived my situation. I knew that if my circumstances didn't change for the rest of my life, I would be fine. I started to enjoy grocery shopping. Lauren was my little helper while Luke would sit shotgun in the cart. Luke would often drive me crazy by pulling food off the shelves if I parked the cart to close to them.

He usually just tried to put the food in his mouth but a few times at checkout I found things he had put in the cart. A few times, it wasn't till I got home that I found what was on his shopping list.

October first was the opening of deer season. My parents made the trip from Elwood so that I could get out in the woods. It felt great to escape everything and sit alone in all that God created. It was my first evening hunting on my dream property when a small deer came meandering through the woods towards me. I just sat quietly and watched as it made its way past. It was a special moment to experience seeing my first deer on my dream property during hunting season. I wasn't able to hunt much that season but that deer was the only deer I would see on the property all season long.

It was now October 13th, and it was Luke's second birthday. His party was to be at the church. I didn't have to do any planning whatsoever as Angela from church, had so graciously, taken care of it all. The kids and I got dressed and out the door we went. I was a bit emotional for the day as it was another milestone that Kari would not see but it was different this time. I wasn't overrun with sadness; I just had an uneasy feeling inside. I felt bad for Luke for not having his mom there to celebrate with him. I felt bad that Kari couldn't be there with him. I didn't ask for all this to happen in my life, but that is what I was dealt. It was my new life and I choose to make the best of it.

The party went great. The support and turnout from the church and family and friends was overwhelming. They had invited everyone from the church nursery so there were a lot of kids there. My family made the long trip from Elwood. Joel and Desiree made the long trip from Lafayette. I was surrounded by so much love and kindness. It was truly a special day for us all. After everyone sang happy birthday, Luke blew out the candles on his cupcake and made quick work of his treat, somehow managing to get most of it in his mouth. After the cake and ice cream, we quickly moved into present time. I stood there with Luke and helped him get the presents open. While I was helping him unwrap, I looked up and saw Fawn walk in. She was clear across the large gymnasium at the church but our eyes met and we smiled at one another. I noticed she was wearing a Payton Manning football jersey, my favorite player, so she instantly had favor in my heart. It felt really strange but I noticed more about Fawn on that day. For the first time, I noticed how beautiful she was.

I also got to meet Fawn's kids. When I met her three year old son Connor, he walked straight up to me and wanted me to hold him. After I picked him up, he looked into my eyes as if saying, I don't know who you are but you seem pretty cool. He then looked around at all the sights happening at the party. Soon he wanted down and he went to my dad standing next to me. My dad picked him up, held him for a bit, and then put him down. Fawn could not believe the actions of her son and said he doesn't usually like to be around men. Maybe he just wanted a bird's eye view of all the excitement but to me, it felt like something different. I felt he somehow knew more.

The next few weeks Fawn and I exchanged a few emails and phone calls. She began to tell me about her hurts from her past and I shared with her the pain that I had gone through. We both shared our passions and her dreams and how God had worked in our lives. As the days past, we started to get to know each other a bit more and it was great to have a friend to talk to. As Halloween drew closer, I was unsure what to do with the children. I had always loved the tradition of trick or treating but I didn't really know many places to take them. I emailed Fawn and asked her if she was going to the church party on Halloween or taking her kids trick or treating. After hearing she was just going to the church, I decided to do the same and we ended up all going to the party together. It was quite the sight, seeing all seven of us loaded in her van with all the kids dressed in costumes. Fawn and I went to that party as friends but we left that party as a bit more.

I had Fawn and the kids out to our house the first week of November for supper. The kids sat down for a movie while Fawn and I prepared the food. There were a lot of smiles that night. We couldn't take our eyes off each other. Things had continued to progress quickly and I knew where things were headed. We had 'the talk' that night in the kitchen and we decided that we would see each other exclusively. I was at complete peace with where everything was at. I had no second guesses. I felt no guilt or shame. Everything just felt right. It was truly a God thing.

That next week, Lauren, Luke, and I went to Fawns place. It was a small apartment, in a large apartment building that she had recently moved into. Fawn had just gotten off work and with her busy schedule; we had decided to pitch in for carryout pizza for supper. We were to meet at the apartment around 5pm. Fawn was just walking into the building when we pulled into the parking lot and she looked back and smiled as she saw us pull in. I unbuckled Luke from his car seat, and carried him inside with Lauren following closely behind. After finding the correct apartment number on the door, we knocked and Fawn told us to come on in. Upon entering the door, I saw Fawn standing at the counter with a large pair of scissors, cutting a piece of pizza into what must have been a thousand pieces. She then proceeded to dump the thousand little pieces of cheese smothered, sausage pizza onto the table top of baby Ally's high chair. Nine month old Ally grabbed for the pizza and stuffed it into her mouth with joyful glee. As I stood with my wide eyes and a perplexed look on my face, I couldn't help but think of the old classic movie Mr. Mom, with the memorable movie quote, "You fed a baby chili?" I asked Fawn if it was OK that she was eating that and she said without hesitation, "Oh yeah, she eats it all the time." I continued to watch baby Ally clean the remaining pieces of pizza of her table top with a bit of nervousness and concern.

When we had finished eating, I noticed a book sitting on the end table next to the couch. I picked it up and read the front cover. Dave Ramsey's Total Money Makeover. I skimmed through the pages with a bit of skepticism. I knew I was good with money. I knew I had things under control. As I sat the book back down, something inside me said I should read it. I picked it up and asked Fawn if she minded if I borrow it. She said sure and told me someone had bought it for her when they had heard of her financial struggles and she hadn't gotten around to reading it yet.

I left her apartment that night with Dave Ramsey on my brain. I got the kids to bed, and quickly started to digest the book. With each page that I turned, my eyes started to widen. The books ideas were so incredibly simple yet so very seldom put into practice. It was not how I was living. According to the book, I was doing it all wrong. I read late into the night that night and finished the book early the next day. I was excited with all that I had learned and I was ready to change my ways. The book reminded me that the borrower was slave to the lender and I didn't feel like I was honoring God by living beyond my means. I needed to slow down and pay for things as I could afford them and quit buying into the idea that a credit score was meaningful.

I quickly began selling things to reduce my debt burden. I sold my truck, my boat, Kari's van, and I cancelled my cell phone. If it wasn't bolted down, I tried to sell it. I quickly reduced my debt burden until nothing was owed for but the house. I felt relief and a weight was lifted from my shoulders. I had enough stress in my life; it felt good to have financial peace. I could sense that Lauren was starting to get nervous as things she had always known to be around, were suddenly gone. I explained to her why we were doing it but I knew it still bothered her. I couldn't help but feel like Lauren was losing some of her security blanket. Life has already changed for her so much in the past couple months. I felt bad for her but I knew I was making the right choices for my family.

Things continued to move quickly in our relationship. We started seeing each other daily and we had fun just being together. It seemed we were complete opposites but at the same time, perfect for each other. Her strengths were my weakness and my weaknesses were her strengths. The kids had adjusted well to each other and they enjoyed the time they got to play together. By December, we started tossing the idea of marriage around. We talked about how fun it would be to have a big family. We started planning a summer wedding for the following year and our excitement and anticipation grew. I bought Fawn an engagement ring and placed it on her hand while sitting in her van in a parking lot. It was not the most romantic of proposals but Fawn was too excited to care. As we drove down the road she began calling family and friends to tell them of the news. It felt as if I were dreaming of how things had changed so fast. I went from the deepest, darkest place I had ever been in, to on top of a mountain in six months. Life was exciting again.

Right after the New Year, I hit a rough spot. It wasn't specifically about Kari; I just started having some feelings of guilt and shame. I had doubts that I was making the right choices. I was having doubts that I was ready to give my heart away completely. I wasn't sure if I was just scared of getting hurt again or if I really wasn't ready. I talked to Fawn about it and told her I needed to pray about it for a couple days and pray

I did. I spent countless hours in prayer seeking his wisdom and answers. I devoted my every free moment to seeking him. To be honest, there was no magic moment for me when I was praying about what I should do. There was no specific bible verse that I read and there was no special message that I heard. I simply prayed that God let me know what to do and that he give me certainty to make the right choices. In those two days that I prayed on it, I went from a confused, doubting person, to someone that knew without a shadow of a doubt, that it was the right thing to do. I can explain it only as a God thing.

On Wednesday January 17th, I called Fawn and asked her what she was doing this weekend. She said, "I don't know, why?" I said, "Do you want to get married?" She was filled with shock and excitement and she emphatically said yes. She had made a list of what she wanted in a husband when she was a teenager and she knew when she met me, I was everything on her list. She felt we were brought together by God as did I.

We immediately started calling family and friends to let them know. I remember talking to my sister Jenna and she asked me if I was crazy. I knew there would be opposition of me getting married so quickly. I knew people would think I was making bad choices and that I wasn't thinking clearly because of my grief, and that I was just acting out of loneliness. I knew people would not understand but only I knew I was healed. I laughed at the 'experts' that said to wait a year minimum before remarrying. I would never put a time on what God can do. His time is different than our time. I asked him to take my pain away and he did. I asked him to mend my broken heart and he did. I felt led by God in the early days after the accident, that I would meet a single mom that needed my help and that is exactly what he gave me. Everything felt so right. I was so thankful for everything he was giving me.

The next couple of days were hectic as we had so many things to do before we could say I do. On Friday, after running around and making many phone calls, we realized it was all going to work out. The next day we would be getting married. That night I had Fawn go home by herself and I kept her kids for the night. I wanted the bride to be well rested for her wedding day. You could sense an excitement with the kids that night. They were very excepting of what was happening. They loved spending time together and they played well together until bedtime. Around 10pm, I got them tucked in bed and headed to my room where I anxiously lie in bed, eagerly anticipating the next day.

I knew without a doubt I was marrying the right girl when she arrived on my doorstep early Saturday morning with a scrub brush in hand. With all the people we had coming over to the house, she wanted to be sure everything was clean. There in the bathroom, just hours before getting married, she stood wearing rubber gloves, and scrubbed down the toilet. Soon after the house was clean, we quickly got ready as we were expecting my parents anytime. I had just finished up in the bathroom when my mom and dad knocked on the door. With a smile on their face, and hands filled with sacks, they walked through the front door. On the way to our house, they had stopped at the store and bought decorations, nuts, mints, toasting glasses, and even an Indianapolis Colts cake to serve as our wedding cake. Fawn and I couldn't believe that on such short notice, they had been so thoughtful for our special day. We were amazed at the love and kindness our family had shown us.

As we stood in front of the kitchen sink with guests all around and kids everywhere you looked, Fawn and I looked into each other's eyes and just couldn't stop grinning. We had come so far in such a short period of time. We felt crazy but at the same time, we felt so right. We knew without a shadow of a doubt that it was supposed to be this way. We had both given ourselves to God and let him take complete control. We couldn't argue with what he was doing in our lives. Fawn stood there wearing jeans, a sweater she had borrowed from her best friend, and no shoes. In the excitement of it all, she had taken her shoes off and had forgotten to put them back on. It was the perfect representation of who she was. There was no fairy tale dress. There was no three tier cake with a fountain and pretty lights. This was real and genuine.

After a quick speech by the mayor of Greencastle, we said our vows and were pronounced man and wife and kissed. It was a surreal moment for us. Our joy and excitement were overflowing. We couldn't stop laughing and smiling. We couldn't take our eyes off each other. All our planning for the wedding was thrown together in two days but God had spent a great deal of time on us and he had worked this out long ago. He brought together to once, very broken people that had their dreams smashed, and gave them a new dream; a dream that would prove to be brighter, larger, and more powerful than ever before. From our once brokenness, came a deep appreciation for what we had. We both felt a love deeper than we had ever experienced before.

The house instantly went from just Lauren, Luke, and I, to a family of seven. It went from a pretty quiet house to a house of chaos. Ally was eleven months old, Luke was two, Connor was three, Becca was five, and Lauren was six. The assimilation of these five kids with their different backgrounds and personalities proved to be a bit difficult and the navigation of providing stability and peace to a blended family was not easy. It was a learning process and we had to rely on God to get us through. I had never wanted a big family but God had different plans for me. I welcomed the new challenges and I was excited at the opportunity to mold and shape the lives of three additional children. I was excited to have another baby in the house. I was excited to be able to teach them about what was important in life. I cherished the opportunity to teach them about God.

Proverbs 18:22

He who finds a wife finds what is good and receives favor from the LORD. (NIV)

CHAPTER 8

OUR NEW LIFE

When I stop and think about this story, I can't help but see how God's hand was at work bringing Fawn and I together. Kari and I had just started attending a new church in Greencastle. It was a church we were highly optimistic about. I had no reason to change churches and had it not been for a selfless act by Stephanie Dinn, I would have continued to attend there. But God had different plans for me. He knew my story before it was written or you could say he wrote it before it happened.

Fawn had experienced quite the pain in her life. Without going into the details of her own personal story, she had what most would consider a difficult childhood. Because of her past, she had learned to shut down as a coping mechanism and this often caused a strain in her relationships. She was raised in church and was a strong believer in God. But like me, she allowed herself to wander off the path and after making some bad choices, she found herself a single mom. She was struggling to keep up with her three kids and struggling to financially make ends meet. She had not been living the life she knew she should have been and in the process, she had buried away her talents.

When she was all alone and in her valley, she turned to God. She began praying feverishly that she make good choices and that he give her strength to go on. She prayed for a Godly man to come into her life. She prayed for help. She began counseling with the minister's wife at our church and she began the healing process. She hoped one day she could begin a ministry to help other women that had found themselves lost in a hurtful and scary world. Around this time, I rolled into town. Angela from church was in charge of organizing the church meals for my family and she asked Fawn if she wanted to contribute. I will never begin to understand how God chooses to do what he does but I can't help but laugh when I think about the situation. God clearly put it upon Angela's heart to ask Fawn for her help. Here Fawn was beaten and broken, living with her parents and with not a penny to her name but Angela asked her to help anyway. Fawn's heart went out to us when she heard about the tragedy and she jumped at the opportunity to help. When I received that email from Fawn in the library, I was incapable of feeling romantic feelings toward someone else but I knew deep down, there was something there. I knew she was special. It is hard to describe what I felt. I was so torn with grief and pain but at the same time, I knew God was at work. Call it destiny, fate, or just call it God's plan. God made all the conditions right. He planted the seeds. He brought the rain. It was only a matter of time before we were ready, and then he knew it would grow into something special.

I don't know why God let's bad things happen to his children. Some say it's because we live in a sinful world. Some say he just stands back and lets things fall where they may. I remember an email that Fawn sent to me in the infancy of our friendship. She shared a bible verse with me that really hit me. It was **John 9:3 "Neither this man nor his parents sinned," said Jesus, "but this happened so that the works of God might be displayed in him."** I found this verse very comforting. I no longer felt like a victim but I felt honored. I was honored that God choose me to display his mighty works. I knew I needed to be a shining light in this dark world. I began praying about that a lot. My hope was that people would see God through my strength and perseverance.

It wasn't long after we had gotten married when I started hearing things. Fawn and I both had people talking about us. Fawn was the evil one preying on an innocent, wounded man while he was grieving, while I was a wounded man, too emotional and too confused by my grief to make any rational choices in my life. I knew people would say it was too soon. I knew a lot of people would say I was lonely and weak, and that I couldn't be alone. But beneath the surface, below what human eyes could see, something beautiful was taking place. God was answering the prayers of two broken people that he had recently pieced back together. I was given everything I prayed for and could have ever asked for in my new wife Fawn. She was given everything she prayed for and had ever wanted in me. Our lives came together not by chance or by circumstance. It was part of His plan.

Before Fawn fully committed to God and allowed him to bring us together, she was in debt, she was working two jobs, and was struggling to find hope. She had little direction in her life. She is now a changed person. Fawn now sings regularly in the worship team at church with the beautiful voice that God gave her. She had locked her singing voice away for so long during the difficult years of her life, but now, like a beautiful flower, she is at full bloom.

She has found a new passion for life by helping others. Just over three years ago she decided to embark on a journey that would take her back to school. She stepped out of her comfort zone and committed herself to do something she never thought possible. After years of grueling hard work, she graduated from nursing school and received her Registered nurse license. As I write this book, she just got her dream job at the hospital where she wanted to work. She is full of life and can't stop smiling from all the blessings she is receiving from God.

As for myself, my passion to help others has continued to grow since we got married. The excitement to write this book has been growing in me for the past year. I always felt God tugging on me to write it but it got to the point I couldn't resist anymore. I knew that even though I was extremely busy, I had to find the time to share my story. Through Fawn's encouragement, proofreading help, and loving support, my dream to write a book is becoming reality. The last three years or so I have devoted a lot of my time to help others achieve their weight loss and fitness goals. My fascination with how the body works has led me on a road of discovery that has had me reading everything I can get my hands on in regards to metabolism, hormones, and wellness. I have spent countless hours trying to soak it all up and I try to share my new found knowledge with anyone that is willing to listen.

This past spring Fawn mentioned that I should go back to school so that I could use my passions in my career. I have always wanted to be in the medical field and felt like that is where I belonged. Somehow, I let my passion and my potential fall through the cracks for many, many years. Fawn inspired me to follow my dream. In one month, I start my journey. I will leave my comfortable life behind, and I to, will go to nursing school. I couldn't be more excited for my life right now. I couldn't be more excited for what lies ahead.

Since Fawn and I have gotten married, great things have been happening in our lives but we wouldn't have expected anything less from something that God brought together. Individually we have changed. Together we have grown stronger. We have our own dreams and we work daily to make them reality. It has been fun to watch and a joy to experience. Our love continues to grow stronger and God continues to pour his blessing upon us. Our blended family has evolved into something truly unique and special. I am reminded of how very special my children are when I hear other people complementing them on their manners in public, when I glance at their report cards and see the effort they put forth, or when I hear them talking about God.

I am also reminded daily of what a gift I have in Fawn. I couldn't have asked for a better wife and best friend. She brings out the best in me and allows me to be who God created me to be. I am blessed beyond measure. I have no doubts, as time moves forward; things will only continue to get better and better. When God brings something together, and when you stay focused on Him, you receive blessings that are beyond even your most imaginable dreams.

God willing, this story is far from over. As I write this book, it has been seven years since the accident. How time has flown by as I still recall it all so clearly. Fawn and I's marriage has been one of ups and downs like any marriage but the opportunity that God gave me to have a new life with one of his children, has been a huge blessing on my life. Our love grows stronger by the day and I couldn't be any happier with how things have turned out. I have no regrets. I have no second guesses. I am happier now than ever before. God has opened my eyes to things I was blind to before. I see things so much clearer now.

John 9:25

"I was blind but now I see!"

CHAPTER 9

WINNING

I was blessed with the opportunity to share in Kari's life. Through our nine years of marriage and a couple more in courtship, I was taught a great deal. I didn't know it at the time, but I was inspired by her. Her passion for life and her passion for Jesus was evident in everything she did. When I think about my time with her, I see the man I used to be and I praise God for the work he has done in me.

Kari's passion was evident with how she lived her everyday life. She never wavered, she never changed, she just was who she was. I recall one day when she got home from driving her school bus, she told me about this young boy she had been talking to. He had been in trouble several times on the bus and had been having disciplinary problems at school as well. She could sense this boy was having problems at home and was having problems with stability and with having a hope in his life. She couldn't help but share with him the hope she had in her life. Without hesitation or reservation, she started talking to this boy about Jesus right there on the bus. When she was telling the story to me, I couldn't help but get upset. I knew the possible ramifications of her actions and I knew we were counting on her income. After voicing my concerns and talking with her about the possibility that she could lose her job for doing that, she paused for a second. She looked at me and simply said, "I don't care. He needed to hear about Jesus."

Another time, she had made the ten minute trip into town to get some groceries and some gas for the lawn mower. It was a Saturday afternoon and we had planned on getting the three acres mowed later that day. As she was nearly home she noticed a young woman with her child, pulled over on the side of the highway. Without a second thought she pulled over and asked if they needed help. They had run out of gas and were stranded with no phone and no way to get help. Kari ran back, grabbed the gas she had just gotten, and poured it into their car. When Kari arrived home, I went out to the van to get the gas so I could start mowing. She met me coming out the door and told me the story of what had happened. She was smiling from ear to ear that she had the opportunity to help someone. My reaction couldn't have been more different. I was angry and upset that she had stopped on the highway as I always felt someday it was going to get her in trouble as it was a recurrent thing she did. I was mad that I didn't have what I needed. I was irritated that my plans for the day had changed. Even though I had grown up in church and felt like I had a relationship with God, this selfless giving was hard for me to understand. It wasn't who I was and I couldn't relate. It seemed I was just going through the motions of life, or at least just going through the motions in my Christian walk. I was not fully committed. I wasn't living for a purpose.

After Kari's accident, I was faced with an incredibly difficult task and it was one that I didn't ask for. I had choices to make. I could choose to die, which certainly would have been the easy choice as I felt I was just a few feet away, or I could choose to keep living, keep fighting, and live with the hope that God had big plans in store for me. I prayed daily that God would mold me, shape me, and change me. I wanted to be a shining light for him. I wanted to make an impact on other people's lives.

Through all my grief and prayer, God did change me in so many ways. I was no longer the selfish man I used to be. My perspective on life changed. I felt as if I was given Kari's eyes and a piece of her heart. I now understood why she did what she did. I now saw what she saw. In a way, I felt closer to her than ever before.

The pain that I felt while in the valley is indescribable. At times I hurt so bad I no longer wanted to live. I hurt worse than I thought was possible. But there is one thing that happens when you experience such an intense pain. All of your senses get magnified. Because I felt the deepest, most hurtful pain imaginable, I could now experience a greater joy than I had ever thought possible. It's as if going through hell has allowed me to see a bit of heaven. I see the beauty of God in all his creation. Simply looking at his birds, his trees, and his clouds brings me joy.

As painful as the past six months had been, I felt honored to have gone through it. God choose me to go through the tragedy because he knew I could handle it and that I would emerge from it stronger than ever before. I am thankful that he chose me. I will not let his story go untold. He changed me in so many ways. My whole perspective on life changed. Small things no longer matter. Things like the weather no longer get me down. Rain, snow, sleet, or hail, my mood always stays the same. Every day is a gift from God and I treasure every gift he gives me. When your joy comes from God, it cannot be taken from you. It just always is. I learned materialistic things no longer matter. I used to want a fancy house and fancy car but now I could care less. I know those things don't bring happiness. Those things really mean nothing. I found my need for those things were only stemming from the hole I had in my heart where God was supposed to be. He became my food. When he is there, I crave nothing. I realized we are here to please God. It's not the other way around. I realized that when you truly live for God, amazing things happen in your life and it's only when you turn away from God, life gets hard. I find this amazingly simple yet so hard to put into practice sometimes. It is so easy to grow cold in your faith. I learned about the precious gift of time. I have realized since the accident that every day is a gift. Kari and I had so many hopes and dreams for our future. We had finally realized our dream and it had only just begun. Kari was twenty nine years old when she went to be with God. As she awoke on June 27, 2006, she had no idea her time was almost up.

Kari wanted God to use her life to further his kingdom but God also used her death in ways just as powerful. It is my hope and prayer that God uses me too. Her impact on my life has made me who I am and it has caused me to look deep within myself to find out who I really am. I am now full of hope and full of purpose. I expect more of myself and I no longer do anything half way. It is my hope that I can inspire others to be the best they can be. To no longer live without hope, but to live their lives to the fullest, live for God, and to follow all of their dreams, no matter if their dreams have been shattered or just lost. God clearly created a burning desire in all of us to have dreams. Living without dreams, is akin to the feather drifting in the wind. You don't have any control over where you are going and you don't know where you will end up. A life with no dreams and no purpose is no life at all. Most of us have had dreams since we were little children. We have big plans for life and then life happens to us. Starting in childhood, daily we are bombarded with little attacks on us. These attacks could be a bad choice of words by a parent or it could be a classmate picking on us at school. At the time, we don't give these interactions much thought, but over time these negative attacks start wearing on us and they change who we are.

As a child, we thought anything was possible. As the years go by, we start losing confidence and we start to gain fear. We lose interest in our dreams because we feel they are so out of reach and so unattainable. We start just going through the motions of life. We look forward to our favorite episodes of reality TV and our dreams are reduced to desperately hoping we someday win the lottery.

We begin to play the victim. We get quite jealous when we here of someone else's success and we say it's because they are lucky. We think if it weren't for bad luck, we would have no luck at all. We live vicariously through extravagant lifestyles in movies. We feel like we got the short end of the stick if we were lucky enough to get any of the stick at all. Somewhere along the way, after being beaten down and broken beyond what we could handle, we took our God given talents and dreams and buried them. These unused talents are the difference between mediocrity and success. God speaks clearly about this very subject in the parable of the talents in **Mathew 25: 14-30.** The servant told his master he was afraid so he buried his masters gold in the ground. His master replied, *"You wicked and lazy servant."* Verse 28-30 is God speaking to us. [28] *"'So take the bag of gold from him and give it to the one who has ten bags. [29] For whoever has will be given more, and they will have an abundance. Whoever does not have, even what they have will be taken from them. [30] And throw that worthless servant outside, into the darkness, where there will be weeping and gnashing of teeth.'*

We are all made for a purpose. That purpose is to worship and glorify God through our talents that he gave us. The more we use our talents to glorify God, the more we will be given. Even those that appear to have the least have their purpose, and when they use their talents, they glorify God. God does not make mistakes.

We are all made to be winners. We are all made to be great. What separates the winners from the losers? A winner uses his potential and a loser buries his long before he dies.

In the parable, what stopped the servant from doing something with the talent he was entrusted with, fear. Fear is crippling and fear is not from God. Fear prevents you from being your best. Fear causes you to take the path of least resistance and the path of least resistance never takes you where we want to go. **Romans 8:31** says **"If God is for us, who can be against us."** No matter how far you fall or no matter what mistakes you make, God is always by your side. You cannot push him away and you cannot make him not love you. If knowing you cannot push away or stop the love of the God of the universe no matter what you do, does not take away your fear, nothing will; for if you know God, there is nowhere to fall but into his open arms, if you fail.

Where did you bury your talents? Do you even know what your talents are? The answer to these questions is incredibly simple. It doesn't matter. To glorify God, you simply be the best you can be in everything you do. The journey will take care of itself once you realize the only stipulation is to give all. We as human beings, created by God, are capable of so much more than we realize. We are born with endless potential that few people even begin approaching by the time they reach their deathbeds. To reach your potential, you must have a purpose for your life and you must work like mad to reach it.

We must ask ourselves, are we just wandering around aimlessly or are we going in a specific direction. If we are going in a specific direction, is the direction even a direction we want to go? I have spent parts of my life wandering around like a feather in the wind, going wherever the wind took me, even if it was not the direction I wanted to go. I know from experience, the life on autopilot is not fun. After Kari died, I was on autopilot for some time. I was just existing and that was part of the reason it was so hard on me. There was nothing to work towards and nothing to look forward to. I had always been a planner. I was always setting goals. But now I had no goals. I had no ambition. I didn't even think I had a life anymore.

A few weeks after the accident, I started having an interest in reading. Once my sister Jenna heard I was reading grief books, she flooded my mailbox with them. I must have read fifteen different books, some multiple times. I was hungry for answers. I was hungry for comfort. Those books gave my life purpose. My purpose was to hit my grief head on. I know without a shadow of a doubt, that finding my purpose helped my grieving process immensely. I wanted more than anything to heal so I poured everything I had into it and with the help of God, it worked.

I want to share a story I heard about a few years ago. Some people say it's a true story. Others say it's an urban legend. Either way, it illustrates a good point about the power of the mind.

John was a large muscular man and he was a hard worker. Some may even say he was the hardest worker at the railroad yard. But no matter how hard John worked, it seemed he never gained ground. He always felt he got cheated. Even though he had no proof, he believed his raises were smaller than his co workers and he always got angry at raise time. Despite John's great work ethic he was a very negative person. He always believed the worst was going to happen.

One summer day while working in the railroad yard, John's boss came around and asked him if he could work overtime to finish up a few things. John really wanted to go home and was not surprised when his boss came around and ruined his evening. As John made his way over to the West side of the yard where his work was to be completed, his mind was filled with negativity.

So much so that he wasn't paying attention to what he was doing.

It was common knowledge at the railroad yard, that upon entering a refrigerated box car you must take extreme caution if you have to enter one for any reason, as the doors would sometimes inadvertently lock on you. With John so focused on how his day was ruined, he had forgotten to disengage the locking mechanism as well as to not completely close the large steel door as he slammed the door shut with anger. John didn't know it at the time but the boxcar had been brought into the rail road yard for maintenance.

John quickly realized what he had done and frantically started beating on the steel door of the boxcar. He hit that door again and again and screamed as loud as he could scream but no one ever came. John soon gave up when the pain of hitting the door had become too much. He realized that his co workers had already gone home for the day and that no one was going to find him.

With his back now against the door, he slowly slid down to the floor of the car. He pulled his legs in to his chest and put his arms around his legs trying to stay warm. John guessed the temperature was well below freezing and dressed in only a short sleeved shirt, he knew if he didn't get out of there, he would freeze to death. The more he thought about it, the colder he got.

About this time, John's boss started wondering if John had left because he hadn't seen him in quite some time. John always walked to work as he didn't live far so there would be no car sitting in the parking lot to leave a clue that he hadn't left. His boss made his rounds, even walking right by where John sat freezing. Had John not given up so easily, surely his boss would have heard him inside the car.

As the end drew near, he thought about his wife and children. He hated that he couldn't say goodbye to them. With frozen, shaking hands he reached into this shirt pocket and pulled out a pen. He frantically looked through his pants pockets for an old receipt to write on but his pockets were empty. He tried to write on the floor of the train car but the pen would not write on the rough surface. With no other place to leave his message, he turned his left hand over and wrote a message on his palm. "So cold. This is the end. I love y"

The following day, as the maintenance crew opened the boxcar to begin their work, they found John lying motionless in front of the door. He was dead. Upon the completion of the autopsy, it was revealed that John, did in fact, freeze to death. Investigators came out to the yard to find that the refrigerated box car that John died in was not refrigerated at all and was broken, and that it had not been working for some time. The low temperature the night of John's death was fifty five degrees Fahrenheit. John froze to death, not because he was freezing but because he thought he was freezing. He expected the worst. He expected to die. He lost all hope and because he thought the worst, the worst happened.

In the same way that John feared the worst, we can also expect the best. If you expect the best, you will be your best. You can create whatever outcome you see in your mind. If you see failure, you will fail. If you see victory, you will be victorious. **Proverbs 29:18** states, *"Where there is no vision, the people perish"*. Visualization is kind of like dreaming with a purpose. You imagine what could be and then develop a plan to make it reality. Within this vision, you never see failure or defeat. You only imagine winning, for if you want to win you must plan on winning.

When I was at my worst, in the deepest, darkest moments of my life, I turned to God. He gave me **Romans 8:38** to comfort me. *[28]"And we know that in all things God works for the good of those who love him, who[a] have been called according to his purpose."* He helped me to believe with all my heart I was going to have a life again. About this time, something magical took place. Because I believed it, it starting happening. I slowly started noticing I could still have fun. I found myself smiling more and started focusing more on happy memories with Kari and less about the tragedy. The more I focused on God, the more I believed anything was possible in my life, and the more I knew I would win.

Our life on earth is short. We only have a set number of days and then it's over. Don't live your life for the weekend. I have often heard people talk about weekdays like they are so foul and disgusting. They wake up on Monday morning dreading the day and they can't wait for Friday to get here. But what if you were diagnosed with cancer and lying in a hospital bed with only days to live. How you would yearn to have more of those Mondays back. You would dream about the chance to be able to start a new week and go to work. What once seemed like work would now seem like an opportunity. You would find joy in just living.

In a 2011 study, it was found that the US life expectancy for a man was 75.6 years and a woman 80.7 years. For the average man, this equals 27,594 days on earth which really isn't all that much time. Now if you are to deduct the disgusting weekdays that most everyone loathes, you are only left with 11,793.6 days in a lifetime to enjoy. To take this a step further, most people start dreading Monday on Sunday afternoon and this could quite easily ruin half of their day. If you deduct the half ruined Sundays you are only left with 9,828 days in a lifetime, to fully enjoy. Why only enjoy 9,828 days when you could have the pleasure of experiencing 27,594 days to the fullest. Those 27,594 days are a gift from God. Don't waste them wishing it were Friday. Every day is what you make of it. Find joy in everything you do. Choose to live everyday like it's your last.

In the latest poll, Americans on average watch TV 34 hours a week. Only in a population of smashed dreams and misdirection could so many people be living the lives of feathers. When you have dreams, when you have purpose, there is no empty time to fill in. It has been estimated that reading a 200 page book takes on average right around 3.5 hours. It has been said if you read four books on any one subject, you will be an expert in that subject. Imagine the possibilities if every one of those Americans was reading nine or ten books a week instead of vicariously living through the lives of others. It's not about how much time we have as we all have twenty four hours a day. It's how we use our precious time that makes the difference.

When you wake up each morning you have a choice to make. It is these choices of your daily activity that determine where you will go in life and what kind of success you will have. You decide if you make choices out of fear or if you make choices because it is the right thing to do to get you where you want to go. You decide if your dreams are worth chasing and you decide if you will put in the blood, sweat, and tears to achieve them. If you decide a dream is worth chasing, there is no one that can get in your way. Only you, through lack of confidence, lack of desire, fear, or just plain laziness can cause your dreams to crumble. When you truly want something, no one can keep you from it.

Don't believe the lie that God created Gold, silver, and diamonds for Satan's people. Success is not from the devil. Success comes from using the talents God gave you. Success is seeking God with all your heart as stated in **Mathew 6:33** *33 "But seek first his kingdom and his righteousness, and all these things will be given to you as well."* When you give your all, you glorify God. God created the riches of this earth for his people. He wants you to be all you can be and enjoy all that he created. He wants you to be more than a fence sitter or as he often puts it in the bible, lukewarm. He wants you to reach the potential he gave you. He wants you to dominate every aspect of your life. When you draw close to God, dominating life just comes natural.

On the flip side, when you are stuck in the perpetual darkness of sin, your life energy is zapped. You become unmotivated, you wallow in self pity, your self esteem diminishes, you make poor choices, and you become depressed. These are all gifts from the evil one. Whenever I am close to God, He makes life so much more enjoyable. It simply amazes me that I sometimes fall away from Him.

I know when I have God, I have everything. It brings me instant happiness and life is overflowing with joy. How could I ever walk away from that? At first the question makes no sense to me and then I am reminded there was only one that was perfect and I am not asked to be perfect. I am asked to have faith, to keep trying, and to give my all for his glory and that is what I intend to do. My life is infinitely better when I am walking with God. God explains this very thing in **John 15: 4-5**. *"Abide in Me, and I in you. As the branch cannot bear fruit of itself, unless it abides in the vine, neither can you, unless you abide in Me . . . for without Me you can do nothing"*

I saw God's power first hand as I walked through the valley of death. I was scared, fragile and weak yet God kept me going. As I greeted people at Kari's viewing I remember how hard it physically was to stand there for six hours. I was so tired and weak. But even though physically and mentally I was a train wreck, God worked through me to comfort others. There were a few people that were really struggling with Kari's death and I, through God's infinite wisdom, found the words to comfort them. He gave me strength that was not my own. He brought me out of the valley faster than human minds thought should have been possible.

So what is the secret to life? What is life all about? Some people spend their entire lives looking for the answers only to die before they find what was right in front of their noses. Again, I am not against material possessions but material possessions are not what it's all about. It's not about how successful you are in your career, how many facebook friends you have, how green your lawn is, or how many bathrooms your house has. All the stuff of this world is here today, gone tomorrow. What really matters is what lasts forever. The secret of life is not getting sidetracked by life as to miss what really matters in life, Jesus Christ.

God promises an everlasting life if we choose to believe and follow him. **Romans 5:8** *"But God demonstrates his own love for us in this: While we were still sinners, Christ died for us."* We are promised everlasting life, not by any deed we have done, or for anything we will do. It is God's promise for us merely having faith that our God is the God of the universe and believing with all our hearts that he is Lord and King. If you know him, believe in him, and follow him, you will be successful in everything you do.

I challenge you to not be normal. Some people will say no one is normal but that is not what I am talking about here. I am referring to an attitude. It is an attitude that sets you apart from the average crowd. It is an attitude that makes you not care what other people think. You make choices because they are the right choices not because it's a choice other people want you to make. You wake up each morning expecting to dominate the day and you choose to live every minute of every day to the fullest. You go out of your way to help others and care more about others than yourself. You are a shining light in a dark world. When you walk into a room, you bring hope. You are not normal because you have given your life away. You carry the cross not because you have to, or because it is expected from you. You do it to honor and glorify God.

We do not choose what happens to us in life. Some people seem to get the easy way out while others seem to get beaten down with every step they take. No matter what happens to us, no matter how hard life gets, we always have a choice. We get to choose how we respond. We can choose to die, choose to give up, and choose to turn from God, or we can choose to win. Choosing to win is not always the easiest thing to do but remember the path of least resistance does not lead us where we want to go. We want the winning path. We want the path that will take us up the mountain. Life is so much more rewarding and so much more fulfilling when you take control of your life and keep climbing. There will be obstacles and there will be heartache and pain along the way, but keep climbing. You will get knocked down; you will get knocked back, but keep climbing. You will grow tired and wearing during the ascension but don't ever quit. Find your strength in God and keep moving forward.

When you reach the mountain top, the beauty is breathtaking. The views are picturesque. The love you feel is overwhelming. Take a moment and take it all in but only rest for a brief moment. You will always be just one misstep away from tumbling back down. There will always be something or someone trying to pull you back down. You must continually work hard to stay on top. You must never get complacent or lazy. You must always remember how difficult the climb was and how hard you worked to get there. You must always hold onto God with everything you have. No matter the circumstances, no matter how hard things get, you must always choose to win!

ABOUT THE AUTHOR

Jason Faulstich was born in Elwood Indiana in 1974 but didn't fully awaken until June 27th, 2006. Since then, his passion for life and his passion to help others has led him on a journey to find the answers for the obesity epidemic. His true passion is honoring God by helping those that struggle with losing weight by volunteering as a weight loss coach. In the future, he plans to be a nurse practitioner specializing in metabolic dysfunction. He lives in Greencastle Indiana with his wife and their five children.

Made in the USA
Charleston, SC
14 December 2013